Aji Notes

Strategic Distinctions and

Competitive Business Skills

To Double Productivity, Value and Income

To Fulfill Financial, Career and Business Intentions

In The Fourth Industrial Revolution (IR#4)

TOBY HECHT

Aji Notes: Strategic Distinctions and Competitive Business Skills to Double Productivity, Value and Income (Volume 1 of 4)

Cover art by Annette Wood and Toby Hecht.

ISBN: 978-1-7339330-1-8

Published by:

The Aji Network Intellectual Properties, Inc.
3914 Lichau Rd
Penngrove CA 94951

aji.com

Volume 1

Aji and The Fourth Industrial Revolution (IR#4)

The Fourth Industrial Revolution (IR#4) began in the 1980s when personal computers and, later, the internet came into existence. Since then, businesspeople's computers have become their primary money-making tools.

The problem for businesspeople is that *how* to use their computers strategically and competitively to double their incomes so they can save enough money for 25+ years of old age with their spouse isn't obvious or commonsensical.

When businesspeople use Aji's fundamental strategy and tactics, they fix this problem. Together, the strategy and tactics show them how to increase their incomes and savings enough in IR#4 to live a good life until they are at least 90 years old instead of suffering about the future with their spouse because they lack enough savings.

Using Aji -- *The Aji Source Fundamental Strategy* and the four fundamental tactics used to execute it -- shows businesspeople how to increase their competitive capabilities and advantages with their computers so they can double their productivity, value and incomes.

Businesspeople say using Aji to double their incomes and increase their savings for old age is easy, enjoyable and definitive. It reduces their anxiety about the future, improves their careers and marriages, and opens completely new opportunities to fulfill their financial, career and business ambitions.

*****

This Book's Format

This book is formatted into different sections of notes that are taken from papers written about Aji by Toby Hecht.

They are Aji's most strategic and competitive distinctions and practices.

Except for the section at the beginning of Volume 1 that explains Aji, the notes are in no particular order.

It includes two Tables of Contents:

#1 - A short list of each section's title

#2 - A longer list of each section's content

The author's purpose is to enable you and your networks of employers, employees, colleagues, customers and vendors to learn and use Aji's most competitive, fundamental distinctions and practices easily and enjoyably to fulfill your financial, career and business intentions.

*****

Contents

By Section Title

Full List

Volume 1

Volume 2

Volume 3

Volume 4

Contents

Full List

Volume 1

The Aji Source® Fundamental Strategy 55

The "Aji Action Package"   *112*

The "Aji Action Package"

> *Ambitions, moods, explanations, distinctions, interpretations, intentions, commitments, business practices, outcomes*

What Is an "Action Package"?

Aji Action Package Distinctions

Action and Business Skills Exist in Businesspeople's Language

The Philosophy of Competition, Part #2 of The Strategy

> *IR#4 Orientations, Intentions, Skills and Tactics*

8 Fundamental Action Distinctions Flow in Sequence

> *Notice, Observe, Assess, Design, Craft, Speak, Prepare to act, Act*

"How Much Money Is Enough?" Calculation   *201*

Building the Frame

About the financial and psychological shock…

"How Much Money Is Enough?" Calculation

4 Fundamental Actions IR#4 Businesspeople Use Every Day to Make Money   *213*

Learning, Communicating, Coordinating and Producing

Competitive Learning *to Produce New Outcomes*

3 Fundamental Competitive Learning Practices: Recurrence, Reciprocation and Recursion

Communicating *Explanations, Commitments, Interpretations and Intentions*

Coordinating *Thought and Action*

Producing *New Offers, Practices, Narratives and Strategies That Are Fresh, New, Highly Valued and Scarce Relative to Demand*

"HELP" 225

What Is "HELP"?

It is money.

"HELP"… *is fulfilling any of four intentions:*

Lower costs
Make fulfilling intentions possible
Improve the value of an outcome
Produce outcomes for people

Reality's Operations 235

Reality's Operations

Cause and Effect. That's it. Nothing else is real.

Aji's Hierarchy of Reality's Operations

3 Fundamental Distinctions Businesspeople Use to Observe and Interpret Reality's Operations

Principles, Laws and Mechanisms

Power **249**

Business Is a Game of Power

Competitive Capabilities and Advantages

What Is Power?

Sources, Forms, Categories, Operations, Methods of Accumulating

Sources of Power

Locations from which capabilities can be acquired (a list)

20 Aji Tactical, Strategic and Competitive Distinctions

To Double Productivity, Value and Income

20 Aji Distinctions   *260*

#1 - Top 1% Explanations: DMRVP

#2 - Prerequisites of the Self

#3 - Quit thought and action guaranteed to produce bottom 99% outcomes immediately!

#4 - Hold all your purposes, or intentions to produce outcomes, simultaneously, at all times and under all circumstances

#5 - Fundamental Strategy: The Aji Source Fundamental Strategy

#6 - Coherence with Reality's Operations

#7 - Use Aji as your IR#4 dominant strategy, every day

#8 - Practice competitive learning, every day

#9 - Accumulate power, every day

#10 - Organization, Structure and State

Volume 2

Humility, The First and Most Powerful Orientation   *43*

Humility in Competitive Circumstances

Aji's orientation is ambitious, humble, strategic, competitive.

Forms of Disrespect

To cultivate your humility, avoid disrespect.

Popular Culture and Businesspeople   *60*

Pop Culture and Businesspeople

Pop Culture

Business Culture

There is no good advice in pop culture to help businesspeople compete successfully in IR#4.

Aji is not pop culture.

Characterizations of Action by Popular Culture

5 Fundamental and SIMPLE Commitments and 4 Fundamental and COMPLEX Commitments   *82*

Businesspeople use commitments to make money.

What Is a Commitment?

What Is an Intention?

3 Ways to Design and Offer

5 Fundamental and SIMPLE Commitments

4 Fundamental and COMPLEX Commitments

The Fundamental Concerns   *104*

Human, Marriage, Career and Business Concerns

13 Human
14 Marriage
12 Career
22 Business, including "The Spine"

The Spine of IR#4 Career and Business Concerns   *118*

The Aji Source® Fundamental Strategy   **135**

Strategies and Dominant Strategies   **169**

Volume 3

Aji's Strategic Jargon and Part #5 of The Strategy

Aji's Tactical Pivot

4 Fundamental Categories of Innovation   *60*

How to Design an Offer **80**

3 Ways to Design an Offer

What Is an Offer?

What Is a Transaction?

The 3 Design Methods

#1 - The Simple Method

#2 - The Legal Method

#3 - The Aji Design Method

Aji's Design Method is ambitious, tactical, strategic and competitive.

How Do Human Beings "Make Money"?

5 Ways People Transact

An Offer's Value Is Determined By Its Scarcity

Offers Generate Revenues, Profits and Income

The Aji Design Method   *106*

Value, Marginal Utilities and The Indifference Principle   *184*

Value, Marginal Utilities, The Indifference Principle

What Is Value?

What Is HELP?

What Is a Marginal Utility?

> *3 fundamental competitive advantages businesspeople produce with Aji:*

>> *First to Market*

>> *The Best Design*

>> *The Most Powerful Combination of New Technologies*

What Is The Indifference Principle?

The 4 Sources of Decline

> *The Self, Situation, Narrative (and Mood), Constitution, or Design, of OPNS*

Business Narratives   *220*

Business Narratives Have 5 Parts

5 Skills Used to Produce a New Business Narrative

Business Narratives Are Used to Constitute Business Roles

What Does It Mean to Design, Craft, Speak, Fulfill and Satisfy?

Designing, Writing and Speaking Explanations   *248*

IR#4's Chronic Crisis of Meaning

DMRVP Explained: *Descriptions, Meanings, Relevance, Value, Purposes*

7 Categories of Purposes

DMRVP Explanations Focus Thought, Design and Action

Language, Interpretations, Intentions, Commitments and Practices

Volume 4

How to Design a New Practice

That Is Fresh, New, Highly Valued

And Scarce Relative to Demand

Coping with Risk Tactically, Strategically and Competitively   84

What Is Risk?

5 Fundamental Sources of Threat

10 Different Ways to Cope With, Manage and Reduce Risk

Truth and Different Epistemologies   *104*

The Sales Conversation Strategy For Top 1% Sales Conversations   *243*

What Is a "Sales Conversation"?

The 10 Parts of The Sales Conversation Strategy

Marketing, Prospecting, Greeting, Qualifying, Presenting, Handling Objections, Closing, Re-closing, Fulfilling, Satisfying

Business Planning: The Executive Summary, Part #2   278

Business is a "Game of Power".

What Is Career and Business Planning?

Use Individual Modules…

The Executive Summary

Background About Aji Notes and

Aji Intention Fulfillment Programs (Aji IFPs)

About *Aji Notes*

What Is an Aji Intention Fulfillment Program (Aji IFP)?

How Do Businesspeople and Business Organizations Benefit
When They Participate in an Aji IFP?

Who Learns How to Use Aji?

Why Do They Do It?

What Do They Care About?

About Aji Notes

The purpose of *Aji Notes* is to help leaders and participants of Aji Intention Fulfillment Programs (Aji IFPs), as well as individuals who just read the notes, to increase their tactical, strategic and competitive capabilities, and the competitive advantages they produce with them.

This enables businesspeople who use Aji to:

Double their productivity, value and incomes.

Double their business' enterprise value.

Fulfill their financial, career and business intentions.

Earn and save "enough money" to avoid running out of it with their spouse during 25+ years of retirement.

The four volumes contain a selection of the most important tactical, strategic and competitive notes from aji.com's collection of more than 1,300 papers and 400 videos about Aji that can be used in Aji IFPs.

More about these distinctions, and many others, is easy to find in the courses and programs offered on (1) aji.com, and (2) in Toby Hecht's book, *Aji, An IR#4 Business Philosophy,* available on Amazon.

*****

* * * * *

Who Can Use These Notes to Lead an Aji IFP?

The minimum requirement to lead an Aji IFP Meeting is to know enough about Aji to use these Notes to explain:

#1 - *The Aji Source Fundamental Strategy*'s 12 strategic and competitive intentions to produce outcomes, how they build on one another and why they work in sequence.

#2 - How to design each of the four fundamental tactics used to execute The Strategy:

How to design an (1) offer, (2) practice, (3) narrative and (4) strategy,

… that is (a) fresh, (b) new, (c) highly valued and (d) scarce relative to demand.

* This takes about 100 days in *The Aji Starter's Course* on aji.com.

*****

Aji Intention Fulfillment Programs (IFPs) are a new business practice in which businesspeople meet once or twice a month *to fulfill their financial, career and business **intentions***, especially to *double* their productivity, value, incomes and enterprise values by age 60.

Aji IFPs show businesspeople how to use Aji's dominant, fundamental strategy to fulfill the financial, career and business intentions, especially to earn and save enough money to live a good life with their spouse, including 25+ years of unemployment during their old age.

When businesspeople participate in an Aji IFP, they gradually increase their competitive capabilities and advantages.

Then they use what they learn to steadily increase their ability to design steady streams of new offers, practices, narratives and strategies (OPNS).

They use the new OPNS they design throughout the day to *double* their productivity, value and incomes, and then do it again.

Many business owners and managers in Aji's IFPs use what they learn to lead IFPs in their own businesses and business organizations to double their productivity, revenues, profits and enterprise value.

They use them to (1) *develop* everyone's competitive capabilities and advantages, and to (2) *attract* and (3) *retain* the most serious and competitive employees.

Participants who do not own or manage a business organization often join together and use aji.com, *Aji, An IR#4 Business Philosophy* and *Aji Notes* to work in their own IFP.

Aji IFPs are available:

On aji.com

From individuals who have studied Aji and run their own Aji IFP

In business organizations that use Aji to increase their employees' productivity, value and incomes, and the profits and enterprise value of their businesses

What Is an Aji Intention Fulfillment Program (Aji IFP)?

An Aji IFP is an ***intention fulfillment program***. It helps businesspeople fulfill their ***financial, career and business intentions.***

Its focus is to help businesspeople earn and save enough money to live a good life during the 40 years of adulthood in which people raise their families and the 25+ years of retirement with their spouse.

In them, participants meet weekly, bi-weekly or monthly for two to three hours to increase their competitive capabilities and advantages, productivity, value and incomes, until their intentions are fulfilled.

Aji IFPs are easy, enjoyable and definitive. Just follow the ***Aji IFP Instructions***, which are easy to download from aji.com.

The purpose of Aji IFPs is to help businesspeople fulfill their *ultimate financial, career and business intentions by age 60* when the infirmities of old age begin to appear, or to simply double their productivity, value and incomes, again and again and again.

To fulfill an "ultimate financial intention" such as being able to retire at age 60 with an annual income of $100k, for example, requires $2.5m in savings (not including inflation).

To retire with an income of $200k requires $5m (not including inflation).

In an Aji IFP, businesspeople calculate what their incomes must become to save "enough money" by age 60 to avoid running out of it with their spouse before they die without reducing their current standard of living.

Then, they learn how to:

1. Design their *offers, practices, narratives* and *strategies* (OPNS)

2. Execute *The Aji Source Fundamental Strategy* to increase their productivity, value and incomes

   … until they can earn and save enough money.

Many participants are business owners, executives or managers who also create and run IFPs for employees in their businesses.

In Aji IFPs, leaders and participants use:

1. ***Aji IFP Instructions*** and ***Aji Reflection Questions***

2. *Aji Notes* (Volumes 1-4)

3. *Aji, An IR#4 Business Philosophy*, by Toby Hecht

4. aji.com

They use them to:

Increase their competitive capabilities and advantages.

Double their productivity, value and incomes, and then do it again.

Increase the enterprise value of their business by developing, attracting and retaining the most serious and competitive employees.

Design and execute fresh, new offers, practices, narratives and strategies (OPNS) that are highly valued and scarce relative to demand.

Increase their strategic and competitive capabilities to execute *The Aji Source Fundamental Strategy*.

Aji IFPs are very powerful and competitive. They are quite literally a new "Source of Power" for businesspeople and businesses that could not have existed before computers and the internet.

We've proven for more than 30 years that businesspeople who join an Aji IFP increase their competitive capabilities and advantages, productivity, value and incomes faster and farther, and more predictably, than any course, seminar or conference.

Our conclusion is that sooner or later every serious businessperson is going to lead or join an IFP.

They will use IFPs to learn and use the *new* tactical, strategic and competitive knowledge that computers and the internet make possible so that they can produce a Normal IR#4 Income that is twice as high as the Normal IR#3 Income they used to earn.

Aji IFPs are *ongoing programs* businesspeople join to increase their competitive capabilities and advantages to produce outcomes that fulfill their *financial, career and business intentions.*

Because Aji IFP Meetings can be held online, they can include businesspeople's colleagues, employees, employers, customers and vendors from anywhere in the world.

An Aji IFP uses Aji, or *The Aji Source Fundamental Strategy* and its four fundamental tactics, to help businesspeople increase their competitive capabilities and advantages.

This enables businesspeople who do not have a pension to increase their incomes enough to live a good life with their family now while also saving and investing "enough money" to avoid running out of it with their spouse during 25+ years of unemployment, retirement or old age.

Summary

To lead your own IFP in your business or with colleagues, you need to know:

1. *The Aji Source Fundamental Strategy's* 12 strategic and competitive intentions

2. How to design fresh, new *offers, practices, narratives* and *strategies* that are highly valued and scarce relative to demand

Learning enough about Aji to lead an Aji IFP usually takes *about 100 days* or completing the first half of ***The Aji Starter's Course*** on aji.com (10 assignments with papers and videos).

Once you know The Strategy's 12 intentions and understand why and how they work in sequence, and you know the four tactics used to execute The Strategy,

... use the ***Aji IFP Instructions*** and ***Aji Reflection Questions*** to increase your competitive capabilities and advantages, productivity, value and income.

In an Aji IFP, the leader and participants prepare, meet regularly and work together for 1-3 hours using (1) *Aji IFP Instructions and Reflection Questions*, (2) *Aji Notes*, Volumes 1-4, (3) aji.com and (4) *Aji, An IR#4 Business Philosophy* weekly or monthly to:

1. Learn tactical, strategic and competitive knowledge to increase their *competitive capabilities* and *advantages, productivity, value* and *incomes*.

2. Design and execute steady streams of *offers, practices, narratives* and *strategies* (OPNS) that are fresh, new, highly valued and scarce relative to demand.

3. Design and execute *The Aji Source Fundamental Strategy* using the new OPNS they produce.

4. Assess, deconstruct and anticipate new OPNS produced by local and global competitors in addition to designing them.

5. Interpret the marketplace's changing competitive situations -- the competitive threats to avoid, obligations to fulfill and opportunities to exploit -- caused by (1) global and local competitors, (2) new technologies, (3) changing demographics, (4) economics and (5) politics.

How Do Businesspeople

And Business Organizations Benefit

When They Participate in an Aji IFP?

When businesspeople meet regularly in an Aji IFP for 1-3 hours to increase their ability to think and act strategically and competitively,

> … they learn and develop a new array of competitive capabilities and advantages

> … that enable them to *double* their productivity, value and incomes, and the enterprise value of their businesses.

Businesspeople's new capabilities and advantages are produced as they learn how to execute *The Aji Source Fundamental Strategy* by using Aji's four fundamental tactics, which are how to design steady streams of fresh, new offers, practices, narratives and strategies (OPNS).

*****

How do individuals benefit?

When businesspeople join an Aji IFP, learning how to execute The Strategy enables them to:

1. *Use the "Aji Action Package"*

   Ambitions, Moods, Explanations

   Distinctions, Interpretations, Intentions

   Commitments, Business Practices, Outcomes

   … to double their productivity, value and incomes

   … by exploiting the new tactical, strategic and competitive capabilities made possible by computers and the internet.

2. *Design and execute* their own steady streams of *offers, practices, narratives* and *strategies* (OPNS) that are fresh, new, highly valued and scarce relative to demand.

3. *Increase their competitive capabilities and advantages*, which happens when they execute *The Aji Source Fundamental Strategy* every day, all day.

4. *Double their productivity, value and income.*

5. *Earn and save "enough money"* (millions) to survive, adapt and live a good life while raising their family *and* during decades of unemployment in retirement with their spouse.

*****

How do business owners, executives, managers and organizations benefit from using Aji?

They benefit, first, by attracting, developing and retaining the most serious and competitive employees.

Using Aji's tactical, strategic and competitive knowledge, instead of common sense, increases the productivity, value and profitability of everyone's offers, practices, narratives and strategies. This increases the business' revenues, profitability and enterprise value.

They use Aji IFPs to:

1. *Double their business enterprise's productivity, profitability and value.*

2. *Show employees how to use their computers, computer-driven tools and the internet tactically, strategically and competitively,*

    … instead of with common sense and task orientation,

    … so they can compete successfully in The Fourth Industrial Revolution (IR#4),

    … which is the most rapidly changing, increasingly complex, intensely competitive and technologically advanced global marketplace in history.

3. ***Increase the organization's tactical, strategic and competitive capabilities and advantages*** continuously by executing *The Aji Source Fundamental Strategy* throughout the day, every day.

4. ***Quit using "traditional" IR#3 business orientations and skills*** that are now obsolete and uncompetitive "inferior strategies".

   Using them, especially task orientation, reliance on common sense and making obvious incremental improvements, suppresses businesspeople's incomes.

5. ***Change the organization's action package*** from IR#3's task orientation to one that is strategic and competitive for IR#4:

   Ambitions, Moods, Explanations

   Distinctions, Interpretations, Intentions

   Commitments, Business Practices, Outcomes

6. ***Learn, communicate, coordinate and produce steady streams of fresh, new offers, practices, narratives and strategies*** that are highly valued and scarce relative to demand.

Who Learns How to Use Aji?

Why Do They Do It?

What Do They Care About?

Three groups of business owners, executives, managers, salespeople and individual contributors learn how to use Aji:

1. Businesspeople who understand they need to double their productivity, value and incomes in order to save enough money by their 60th birthday to take care of their spouse and children when they retire.

2. Businesspeople who already have very high incomes, who are rich and who want to become richer.

3. Businesspeople who learn how to use Aji from their managers or business leaders.

The first group is businesspeople whose marriage vows and parenting commitments compel them to earn and save enough money to avoid running out of money with their spouse before they are at least 90 years old.

What marriage vows?

To some spouses, their marriage vows, such as to love, honor and cherish their spouse until death, etc., mean that they cannot sit idly, or be apathetic about, taking care of their spouse's most fundamental human concerns when they grow old.

In their view, they must learn how to earn and save enough money to afford *food, housing, medical care* and *transportation* for their spouse during 25+ years of retirement to keep their marriage vows.

For this group, doubling their incomes and saving enough money to avoid chronic financial stresses later in life is part of their marriage vows and very satisfying. Taking care of their spouse's most fundamental human concerns for survival makes their life deeply meaningful from their point of view.

The idea that they could find themselves unable to afford non-discretionary goods and services their spouse needs to survive, adapt and live a good life in old age such as good medical care and food is *unacceptable* and would produce existential despair as they grow older and become increasingly desperate.

What parenting commitments?

1. *To raise their children so they can earn and save enough money when they become adults to live a good life* with their own families, or to earn a Normal IR#4 Income that is twice as high as a Normal IR#3 Income

   To accomplish this, parents must be able to (1) speak about how to do it and (2) model the behavior every day.

   Learning Aji enables them to fulfill this commitment.

2. *To avoid becoming a "parent tax",* or financial burden, on their children and their children's families when they retire because they failed to earn and save enough money to avoid running out of it during 25+ years of old age with their spouse

The second group is businesspeople who already have very high incomes, who are rich and who want to become richer.

Aji easily attracts businesspeople who are already successful.

We've had MBAs from all the top business schools learn Aji, businesspeople whose incomes are over $10m and business owners worth more than $100m.

They hear about it, check out The Strategy and its four fundamental tactics, and make their choice.

The third group learns how to use Aji from their managers or business leaders because The Strategy is used by the team, organization or business.

The more this group learns about The Strategy and how to execute it, the more they, too, understand how to *double* their productivity, value and incomes.

Their reactions vary. They range from being passionate and serious about using Aji to being mildly interested. A small minority don't like it.

Aji IFPs work very well for these groups in terms of enabling them to increase their productivity, value and incomes, which also increases their business' enterprise value.

IFPs are produced for this group. They won't generate their own.

*****

Background About Aji

What Is Aji?

What Does Aji Mean?

Good and Bad Aji Moves

Full Moves

What Produces "Good Aji" in IR#4?

What Produces "Bad Aji"?

What Happens to Businesspeople and Their Families
During an Industrial Revolution?

About NEW Tools and Knowledge in Industrial Revolutions,
… e.g., Computers and the Internet

What Is Aji?

Aji is a new business philosophy and a new dominant strategy for IR#4,

> *… including completely new business orientations, intentions and skills,*

> *… that enables businesspeople to earn a Normal IR#4 Income*

> *… that is twice as high as the Normal IR#3 Income they currently earn.*

Aji is a business philosophy invented for The Fourth Industrial Revolution (IR#4). Using it enables businesspeople to use their computers, computer-driven tools and the internet tactically, strategically and competitively, instead of with common sense, task orientation and hard work.

Using *The Aji Source Fundamental Strategy* shows businesspeople how to *double* their productivity, value and incomes so that they can earn and save enough money by their 60th birthday to avoid running out of it with their spouse before they are 90 years old.

The Strategy is based in a completely new set of (1) business *orientations,* (2) strategic and competitive *intentions* to produce outcomes and (3) *business skills* to fulfill those intentions.

When businesspeople, or business organizations, learn how to execute *The Aji Source Fundamental Strategy*, it shows them *why, with whom* and *how* to double their productivity, value and incomes easily, enjoyably and definitively.

How to double their productivity, value and income becomes obvious!

To use Aji, businesspeople learn the:

1. *12 strategic and competitive intentions* of The Strategy

2. *Four fundamental tactics* businesspeople use to execute it

    How to design and execute a fresh, new (1) *offer,* (2) *practice,* (3) *business narrative* and (4) *strategy*

    … that is (a) fresh, (b) new, (c) highly valued and (d) scarce relative to demand.

The Strategy and its four fundamental tactics are explained in these notes, on aji.com and in *Aji, an IR#4 Business Philosophy*, by Toby Hecht.

Once businesspeople learn The Strategy and the tactics, *which usually takes about 100 days* or until they finish the first half of ***The Aji Starter's Course***, they can begin to execute The Strategy to fulfill their financial, career and business intentions.

What Does Aji Mean?

The name Aji comes from the strategy game Go, which is a 4,000-year-old game invented in Asia to teach generals how to think strategically.

The word "aji" means "having the potential to win".

Go is a board game. The board is a grid like a chess board with 19 intersecting and perpendicular lines.

Two players alternate placing black and white stones, or pieces, on the intersections created where the lines cross to take territory, or market share in a marketplace.

The player who controls the most territory at the end of the game wins.

Each game requires about 250 moves.

Good and Bad Aji Moves

When players put down a stone that increases the likelihood they will win the game, it is said that they made "a good aji move". A move that does the opposite is called "a bad aji move".

When players are well positioned on the board with competitive advantages, it is said "they have good aji".

When their competitive position is weak or flawed, "they have bad aji".

When businesspeople, and entire business organizations, shift their orientations, intentions and skills with Aji, they immediately begin to produce "good aji" for themselves and their organization by designing and executing steady streams of fresh, new offers, practices, narratives and strategies… instead of simply getting the job done.

Full Moves

A "full move" is the move businesspeople can make in their career or business at any given moment with their offers, practices, narratives and strategies (OPNS),

> … or in any competitive situation, among a dozen or so alternatives,

> … that takes care of the highest number of tactical, strategic and competitive concerns and situations at the time.

The ability to make "full moves" when playing Go is an essential competitive capability to win the game.

> When people make a full move, they produce "good aji" that helps them fulfill their financial, career and business intentions.

When businesspeople execute *The Aji Source Fundamental Strategy,* it shows them how to make full moves with their offers, practices, narratives and strategies.

The immediate increase in businesspeople's productivity, value and incomes when they make full moves with Aji shows that this approach is at least *twice* as competitive as completing tasks and using common sense.

What Produces "Good Aji" in IR#4?

Good aji means businesspeople's thoughts and actions are gaining the competitive capabilities and advantages they need to fulfill their financial, career and business intentions, or to simply double their productivity, value and incomes.

It is created in The Fourth Industrial Revolution (IR#4) by using computers, computer-driven tools and the internet tactically, strategically and competitively, rather than to get jobs done while relying on common sense.

  It's created when businesspeople execute a competitive, fundamental strategy to make money and use them to design and execute their own steady streams of fresh, new offers, practices, narratives and strategies that are highly valued and scarce relative to demand.

Using Aji's (1) *orientations*, (2) *intentions* to produce strategic outcomes, and (3) *new business skills* to fulfill those intentions *produces good aji*. It increases the likelihood businesspeople will compete successfully enough to fulfill their financial, career and business intentions, or to double their productivity, value and incomes.

What Produces "Bad Aji" in IR#4?

Bad aji means businesspeople's thoughts and actions are thwarting their financial, career and business intentions because they lack marginal utilities. As a result, their incomes are only 50% of what would be possible if they used their computer strategically.

It is produced when businesspeople:

Use their computers and the internet to complete tasks instead of executing a competitive, fundamental strategy that increases their competitive capabilities and advantages.

Work with, and listen to, people who rely on task orientation and common sense to make money.

Rely on their common sense instead of a competitive, fundamental strategy.

Are satisfied making incremental improvements, i.e., minor innovations that are mediocre, rather than marginal utilities that are fresh, new, highly valued and scarce relative to demand.

Work, think and plan alone instead of working strategically and competitively with an IR#4 Network of Capabilities.

These traditional IR#3 business skills and task orientations about how to make money are obsolete, mediocre and uncompetitive.

They suppress businesspeople's productivity, value and incomes by at least 100%.

What Happens to Businesspeople and Their Families

During an Industrial Revolution?

I designed Aji as I invented how to exploit the new tactical, strategic and competitive capabilities computers and the internet make possible so that I could earn a living to take care of my spouse and children and, hopefully, become rich.

I accepted the widely held interpretation that global competitors were already using their computers and the internet to produce goods and services whose value was so new, so good and so superior to those produced before computers were invented that a new industrial revolution, The Fourth Industrial Revolution (IR#4), was underway.

Since I had some background studying how industrial revolutions unfold by putting new competitive and financial pressures into play that drive businesspeople and businesses to change how they think and act to make money, had also studied economics, business, competitive strategy, Go, philosophy and linguistics, and had opened the first retail chain for selling personal computers in the country, I had some idea what to expect.

Here is a summary.

An industrial revolution is, fundamentally, *a new competitive situation* *with new competitive threats, obligations and opportunities no one can see or understand*, at first. It is created by the businesspeople who first adopt and adapt to an entirely new category of tool by learning how to use it to produce new offers, practices, narratives and strategies (OPNS) with new standards of value throughout the marketplace.

> Nothing during an industrial revolution about the new competitive situations in which businesspeople find themselves needing to earn a living to take care of their families is obvious, objective or perceivable. No one knows what's going to happen.

> New OPNS, which include new goods and services, are *invented,* and *reinvented*, daily for decades as the industrial revolution unfolds.

> Those who can't, or won't, adapt by learning new orientations, intentions and skills get left behind and are unable to save enough money to afford 25+ years of old age with their spouse.

In IR#4, new competitive situations that are new OPNS are produced throughout the day, every day. They are created by businesspeople who invent how to use a new category of tool such as a computer to increase competitive standards about what is valued so much that they make traditional OPNS created using "old tools" and "old skills" uncompetitive.

Eventually, the financial and competitive pressures and harsh consequences to the families of businesspeople who don't, or won't, adapt and consequently can't make enough money to avoid running out of it with their spouse before they die, force them to adapt.

Learning how to use Aji is a way businesspeople adapt or "pivot" away from IR#3's obsolete skills and pivot towards using completely new orientations, intentions and business skills with their computers and the internet.

Industrial revolutions move in two stages.

In the first stage, businesspeople buy and use the new tools but do not change their knowledge, or the orientations, intentions and skills with which they use them. They continue to use "traditional" business orientations and skills with which they are familiar and that define mediocrity in the new industrial revolution.

> This produces failure and suffering for the overwhelming majority of businesspeople and businesses. It prevents them from making "enough money" to live a good life their entire life, even though they are using computers.

> This is because simply buying new tools and learning how to make them work is easy and obvious, and produces no competitive advantages. Everyone can do it. It has no marginal utility.

> The remedy is always the same:

>> Until businesspeople quit relying on their familiar and comfortable moods and narratives about business and how to make money,

>>> … and acquire strategic knowledge that enables them to fully exploit their new tools,

>>> … they cannot compete successfully against those who do.

In the second stage, businesspeople learn new:

1. *Orientations*, or ways of being, such as *being* strategic, ambitious, powerful and humble, instead of *being* task-oriented, commonsensical, aimless and prideful.

2. *Intentions to produce new outcomes* such as IR#4 Networks of Capabilities and identities of superior trustworthiness, value, authority, leadership and dignity, instead of getting jobs done with common sense, hard work and incremental improvements.

3. *Business skills* that exploit the new competitive capabilities and advantages the new tools have made possible, instead of using their new computers with obsolete intentions and skills, which become "inferior strategies".

This is what using Aji enables.

What are the four industrial revolutions?

IR#1 - Steam-powered tools	1750 - 1830
IR#2 - Electric-powered tools	1830 - 1870
IR#3 - Transistorized tools	1870 - 1980
IR#4 - Computerized tools	1980 - Present

The Third Industrial Revolution (IR#3) ended in the 1980s when personal computers were invented. It was organized around the use of transistorized tools, or *"single-purpose tools" that could only produce one outcome.*

Transistorized calculators and remote controls, for example, as well as shovels and pencils, steam-powered locomotives, electric irons and toasters, *are all single-purpose tools.*

Each one can be used to produce only one outcome. Pencils only make marks. Irons only iron. Elevators only move up and down.

To use single-purpose tools productively and competitively, *people must use task orientation.* Nothing else is possible.

Computers, on the other hand, are *"multi-purpose tools".*

They can be used with task orientation to get the job done.

They can also be used with strategic orientation to execute a competitive, fundamental strategy with completely new intentions and business skills such as Aji, which is *at least* twice as productive and valuable.

When businesspeople use their computers with IR#3's task orientation and common sense, or manage people that way, they *cannot* exploit the new capabilities to learn, communicate, coordinate thought and action, and produce and execute fresh, new offers, practices, narratives and strategies (OPNS) very, very quickly.

The moment businesspeople are shown how to use their computers and the internet tactically, strategically and competitively, which happens when they learn The Strategy's 12 strategic intentions,

> … they immediately see completely new opportunities to increase their productivity, value and incomes

> … that they could not see with their common sense or determination to get the job done.

It's *"easy"* because Aji makes sense, albeit a new kind of sense.

It's *"enjoyable"* because businesspeople enjoy doubling their incomes so they can:

Save enough money to avoid running out of food, housing, medical care and transportation with their spouse during 25+ years of old age

Become rich ($10m capital-at-work)

Become richer than they already are

It's *"definitive"* because when businesspeople use Aji to increase their competitive capabilities and advantages, productivity, value and incomes, they know exactly what they did to succeed and why it worked.

About NEW Tools and Knowledge

in Industrial Revolutions

e.g., Computers and the Internet

At the heart of understanding the nature of industrial revolutions and how to exploit their new competitive situations to earn a living or become rich, rather than succumb to them and fail to save enough money for decades of old age,

> … is understanding the true nature and operations of tool use by human beings.

The media speaks about The Fourth Industrial Revolution (IR#4), which began in the 1980s, as if computers did it.

> This is not true. Computers don't *do* anything. They have no intentions or skills to produce outcomes.

> Smart, ambitious and competitive businesspeople created IR#4 by inventing ways to make money that exploit the new tactical, strategic and competitive capabilities computers make possible.

> One way or another, they quit using IR#3 business orientations, intentions and skills decades ago, and began using a competitive, fundamental strategy instead, such as Aji. Now they are rich.

What's most important to know about industrial revolutions, and remember, is *people, not their tools,* produce them and keep them going by continually inventing new ways to use tools tactically, strategically and competitively to create new goods and services that create new standards for value throughout the marketplace.

In other words, it's people like *you* who produce industrial revolutions. You do it the moment you begin producing steady streams of offers, practices, narratives and strategies that are fresh, new, highly valued and scarce relative to demand, instead of mediocre, and that you use strategically, instead of to get jobs done.

In IR#4, new standards of value -- or what is considered important, useful and worthwhile to buy -- are produced with new OPNS, and new goods and services, throughout the day in as little as 15 minutes.

Aji is a business philosophy that enables businesspeople who continue to use business skills invented long before computers and the internet to quit using them and thwarting their financial intentions forever.

Using Aji enables businesspeople gripped by IR#3 business culture to pivot and learn how to compete strategically and successfully enough to double their productivity, value and incomes.

It shows businesspeople how to exploit the new tactical, strategic and competitive capabilities and advantages their computers and the internet make possible for the first time in history, which are not obvious to common sense,

… so they can see for themselves how to compete successfully.

About Tools

(especially computers and the internet)

People use tools to increase their capabilities to produce practical outcomes they need to survive, adapt as they and their situations change, and live a good life with their family and in society. Designing, producing, using and improving tools is fundamental to human existence.

> The people and businesses who design and build the best tools and invent the best practices to use them to produce outcomes that fulfill their intentions (new technologies), make the most money.

Contrary to claims made on the internet and in the news, tools don't *do* anything. Computers and the internet don't *do* anything. They don't intend to help anyone. They just sit on shelves and desks, or in bags.

> The value of businesspeople's computers is not inherent. It is in the new competitive practices they make *possible* for people to invent when they use them.

> The point is, no tool that is used to make money does businesspeople or businesses any good in a rapidly changing and intensely competitive situation until they learn new competitive capabilities, or invent new practices, that enable them to produce new competitive outcomes that keep up with the speed of change around them.

Tools are not technologies, as popular culture casually claims. They are *devices* people use to produce outcomes to fulfill their intentions.

Hammers are the same as computers in this way. They don't do anything. They don't intend to help anyone.

A hammer's value is in its use or utility. It is the practice of hammering nails to produce highly valued outcomes that their existence makes possible.

If people don't know how to hammer a nail, hammers don't show them how to do it. They don't build anything themselves.

But, when people invent how to use a hammer, the hammer's existence makes it possible for them to significantly increase their productivity, value and incomes.

Technologies are human actions and practices to produce practical outcomes *and not the devices people use to perform them.*

Knowing the difference between devices, which are things, and technologies, which are human practices, changes "everything", especially businesspeople's focuses and the interpretations they make about how to compete successfully.

Technologies are:

1. ***The practices*** people like *you* invent to produce new tools such as computers and the internet.

2. ***The practices*** people like *you* design and execute to exploit the *new* tactical, strategic and competitive capabilities your computers and the internet make possible to make money.

*Understanding this changes **everything**.*

Aji shows businesspeople why and how to produce their own new technologies.

The fundamental reason human beings invent tools is to increase or expand their capabilities to produce practical outcomes that fulfill their intentions.

Tools are usually artifacts such as hammers and computers, but can be found objects as well such as rocks and sticks.

New knowledge is required to build a new tool, by definition, *because it is a new outcome in a given set of circumstances.*

That *knowledge*, or the *practices* people use to produce the new tool, is called a *technology.*

The more quickly new tools such as new computer-driven devices and applications are created, and the faster newer tactics and strategies become possible to invent because of them,

… the faster and more competitively important it becomes for businesspeople and businesses to use their computers and the internet

… to design fresh, new offers, practices, narratives and strategies (OPNS)

… that are highly valued and *scarce relative to demand.*

Summary

"Computer technology" is the:

1. *Practices* people design and use *to make a computer*

2. *Practices* they design and execute with their computers *to produce outcomes*, or new OPNS, including goods and services.

Technologies are never the devices, tools or computers themselves.

Those are artifacts, not human practices.

It is businesspeople who design and execute their own OPNS using their computers and the internet who are producing new technologies.

*****

* * * * *

How to Get Started with an Aji IFP

To Get Started Using Aji Is Easy, Enjoyable and Definitive

How Can You Join an Aji IFP?

How Can You Have Your Own Aji IFP in Your Business?

To Get Started Using Aji Is Easy, Enjoyable and Definitive

The first new skills businesspeople learn with Aji are The Strategy's:

1. *12 strategic intentions* (30 minutes)

2. *Four fundamental tactics*: How to design a new (1) *offer,* (2) *practice,* (3) *business narrative* and (4) *strategy*

    ... that is fresh, new, highly valued and scarce relative to demand (100 days)

Learning The Strategy and its four fundamental tactics reveals*:*

What businesspeople need to do

How they need to do it

Why they need to do it

     ... to *double* their productivity, value and incomes.

     * The tactical, strategic and competitive knowledge needed to use Aji is Part #3 of The Strategy.

One of Aji's immediate benefits is how it enables everyone to naturally quit using obsolete and uncompetitive business intentions and skills invented long before computers and the internet were invented.

It replaces reliance on obsolete business skills, task orientation and common sense that produce mediocre outcomes and Normal IR#3 Incomes with designing and executing steady streams of offers, practices, narratives and strategies, including goods and services, *that are twice as productive and valuable.*

> Common IR#3 business orientations, intentions and skills produce outcomes, OPNS, including their goods and services, that define mediocrity in IR#4.

> Using them in IR#4 suppresses businesspeople's value and incomes by at least 100%.

IR#3's obsolete business skills include:

1. *Hard work*

2. *Task orientation or determination to get the job done*

3. *Reliance on common sense*

4. *Processes and procedures*

5. *Incremental improvements*

For a complete overview of Aji, please read Chapter One of *Aji, An IR#4 Business Philosophy* by Toby Hecht, available on Amazon.

To read a short explanation of The Strategy,

     ... please read Chapter Two.

To read a longer explanation of each of The Strategy's 12 parts,

     ... please read Chapter Six.

There are also two short explanations of The Strategy's 12 strategic intentions in these notes.

How Can You Join an Aji IFP?

To find out more about Aji IFPs, or to join one:

Go to aji.com

Call (408) 730-2234

How Can You Have Your Own Aji IFP in Your Business?

Having an Aji IFP in your business attracts, develops and retains the most serious and competitive employees.

It enables your employees to begin to think and act tactically, strategically and competitively with offers, practices, narratives and strategies they design,

> … and to quit relying on their common sense, hard work and task orientation

> … to help you fulfill your financial, career and business intentions.

This creates moods of enthusiasm, eagerness to learn and compete, and passion for the work and future people are bringing into existence.

Producing your own Aji IFP enables you to:

1. Steadily increase everyone's tactical, strategic and competitive capabilities and advantages, productivity, value and incomes.

2. Make your business more attractive to new hires.

3. Retain and recruit the most serious and competitive employees.

4. Increase the business' enterprise value.

If you are a business owner, executive or manager who wants to create an Aji IFP in your business:

Request to visit an Aji IFP and join one of the monthly meetings. (Guests are welcome.)

If you would like to move forward and learn Aji:

Go to aji.com for offers and instructions.

Start with the *Introduction to Aji Course* or sign up for a subscription on aji.com and do *The Aji Starter's Course*, which is 21 assignments.

Request to join an Aji IFP.

*****

The Aji Source® Fundamental Strategy

What Is *The Aji Source® Fundamental Strategy*?

About The Strategy (short version)

The Strategy produces new CDVF

The Aji Source® Fundamental Strategy

The Strategy's

12 Strategic and Competitive Intentions

(long version)

What Is The Aji Source® Fundamental Strategy?

The Aji Source Fundamental Strategy is a competitive, fundamental strategy with 12 tactical, strategic and competitive intentions that businesspeople fulfill in sequence.

     * The intentions are listed and then explained later in this section.

The Strategy is "competitive" because every outcome used to execute it is designed using Aji as a dominant strategy to produce competitive advantages and "good aji".

     This makes each outcome businesspeople create, or their new OPNS, more productive and valuable by giving them marginal utilities whose benefits are *superior* to competitors'.

Aji is "fundamental" because its 12 intentions underlie and enable the constant production of fresh, new offers, practices, narratives and strategies (OPNS) that are highly valued and scarce relative to demand.

Using The Strategy is one way businesspeople, and entire businesses, can adapt to The Fourth Industrial Revolution (IR#4) so that they are able to *double* their productivity, value and incomes, or earn and save enough money to live a good life with their family, including 25+ years of unemployment during old age.

Using The Strategy enables people and business organizations to adapt to IR#4's rapidly changing competitive situations by:

1. Showing them how to use their computers and the internet tactically, strategically and competitively to produce entirely new competitive capabilities and advantages, orientations, intentions and business skills to fulfill their financial, career and business intentions.

2. Enabling them to *quit* using IR#3's task orientation, common sense, processes and procedures, and incremental improvements that are now obsolete, uncompetitive, define mediocrity in IR#4,

   … and that suppress businesspeople's incomes by at least 100%.

Each industrial revolution (IR) produces new competitive situations in which businesspeople are forced to compete to take care of their families. It is created, and won, by the businesspeople who, regardless of their role, invent completely new ways to think and act to produce outcomes, especially goods and services, with a new category of tool,

> … i.e., steam-powered tools (IR#1), electrical tools (IR#2), transistorized tools (IR#3) and now computer-driven tools (IR#4).

Industrial revolutions are begun when ordinary businesspeople get access to new tools they can use to produce new goods and services whose value is superior to anything produced in the past industrial revolution with older tools.

Gradually, those who create new ways to produce goods and services also create new competitive and financial pressures for everyone else that prevent businesspeople and businesses who have not yet adapted, or who continue to use old business skills, from making enough money.

> This is why most businesspeople are so far behind saving enough money for their old age and are certain to run out of it with their spouse long before they die.

> Using The Strategy is one way businesspeople, and entire businesses, can pivot towards IR#4 and fulfill their financial, career and business intentions.

The consequences produced when businesspeople can't earn and save enough money to avoid running out of it with their spouse after they become too old to work eventually force everyone to adapt.

Psychologists, scientists, doctors, philosophers and economists agree. When human beings face a future without enough money to afford enough food, housing, medical care and transportation,

> ... they experience increasing hardships, desperation, despair, chronic stress, suffering and shortened lifespans.

When businesspeople use The Strategy, they adapt to IR#4. Their productivity, value and incomes *double* because they learn how to use their computers and the internet to produce new competitive capabilities and advantages that are tactical, strategic and competitive, rather than task-oriented.

It's easy, enjoyable and definitive.

After this short introduction, you will find:

> ***#1 - A two-page summary of The Strategy***

> ***#2 - Brief explanations of each of The Strategy's 12 strategic
> and competitive intentions***

Use them to learn each of The Strategy's intentions and why they flow
in sequence to produce new competitive capabilities and advantages
with your offers, practices, narratives and strategies to fulfill your
financial, career and business intentions.

Use them to change your action package, which is the set of (1)
ambitions for your future, (2) *moods,* (3) *explanations* about business
and how to make money, (4) *distinctions,* (5) *interpretations,* (6)
intentions to produce outcomes, (7) *commitments* to customers,
employers, employees, etc., (8) *business practices* and (9) *outcomes*
that you use to make money.

When businesspeople, and business organizations, use Aji's Action
Package, they can double their productivity, value and incomes, and
then do it again.

> You can find a short summary of *The Aji Source Fundamental
> Strategy* in Chapter Two of *Aji, An IR#4 Business Philosophy*,

> … and a longer version in Chapter Six.

About The Strategy

(Short Version)

The Strategy, or *The Aji Source Fundamental Strategy*, is a new way of thinking and acting to make money in a rapidly changing and intensely competitive global marketplace organized around the use of computers and the internet.

It's also a new dominant strategy for IR#4. (This is explained elsewhere.)

The Strategy's purpose and value are located in its ability to help businesspeople use their computers and the internet strategically and competitively to double their productivity, value and incomes,

... so that they can produce a Normal IR#4 Income

... that is twice as high as their Normal IR#3 Income.

To double their incomes, The Strategy specifies and shows businesspeople why and how to fulfill 12 new strategic and competitive intentions every day, all day, instead of using obsolete business knowledge to get jobs done invented for IR#3.

To continue to produce a much higher income, businesspeople use The Strategy, instead of their common sense to complete tasks, which worked in IR#3 but is now an "inferior strategy".

The Strategy is executed using four fundamental tactics: designing and executing steady streams of fresh, new (1) *offers*, (2) *practices*, (3) *business narratives* and (4) *strategies* (OPNS).

The Strategy uses a new set of business *orientations, intentions* and *skills* that shows businesspeople, and entire businesses, how to use and exploit the new strategic and competitive capabilities made possible by computers, computer-driven tools and the internet.

The Strategy is launched in Part #1, Ambitions, when businesspeople constitute their financial, career and business intentions, which must now include having enough money saved to retire by their 60th birthday, which is when doctors say the infirmities of old age begin to appear.

An *Aji Ambition* includes earning and saving enough money to live a good life while raising one's family and saving enough money to afford the goods and services everyone needs to survive, adapt over time and live a good life with their spouse, including 25+ years of unemployment and old age.

The Strategy Produces New CDVF

When businesspeople use The Strategy to formulate their financial, career and business ambitions, their actions create completely new:

1. ***Commitments***   Promises, requests, offers, practices, narratives, strategies,

   … made to customers, employers, employees, colleagues and vendors

2. ***Directions***   What to move towards and away from with one's thoughts and actions (the action package) as new offers, networks, accomplishments, identities, leadership roles, organizations, etc., appear

3. ***Velocities***   The speed, velocity or amounts of accomplishments, money and other outcomes that need to be designed, executed, earned, saved and invested, by when

4. ***Focuses***   What needs to be paid attention to, and what does not, to double productivity, value and income, or to fulfill IR#4's financial, career and business intentions

The remaining 11 intentions of The Strategy show businesspeople, and business organizations, how to fulfill the financial, career and business intentions that they constituted in Part #1.

The Strategy's intentions are tactical, strategic and competitive, and are constituted with new:

1. *Orientations*, or ways of being productive, competitive or valuable

   … such as *being* strategic, rather than *being* task-oriented

2. *Intentions* to produce tactical and strategic outcomes

   … such as producing identities of *superior* trustworthiness, value, authority, leadership and dignity with customers

3. *Business skills* to use with their computers and the internet,

   … such as knowing how to design a new offer that is fresh, new, highly valued and scarce relative to demand

   … that increase businesspeople's *competitive capabilities* and *advantages* very quickly.

This enables businesspeople to fulfill their financial, career and business intentions, or to simply double their productivity, value and incomes.

The Aji Source® Fundamental Strategy

#1 - Constitute *ambitions and business missions*

#2 - Formulate *Philosophies of Care and Competition*

#3 - Learn *tactical, strategic and competitive knowledge* needed to execute The Strategy

#4 - Use *Ethics of Power* to produce competitive capabilities and advantages

#5 - Design *offers, practices, narratives and strategies* (OPNS) that are fresh, new, highly valued and scarce relative to demand

#6 - Build *IR#4 Tactical, Strategic and Competitive Networks of Capabilities* (IR#4 NWC)

#7 - Increase *autonomies, competitive capabilities and advantages*

#8 - Produce *steady streams of accomplishments* that are fresh, new, highly valued and scarce relative to demand

#9 - Establish *identities* of *superior* trustworthiness, value, authority, leadership and dignity (TVAL&D)

#10 - Hold highly compensated *leadership roles*

#11 - Build *business organizations* that are strategic and competitive in IR#4

#12 - Anticipate *future competitive threats to avoid, obligations to fulfill and opportunities to exploit*

The Aji Source® Fundamental Strategy's

12 Strategic and Competitive Intentions

#1 - Constitute and fulfill financial ambitions needed to survive, adapt over time as one's body and circumstances change and live a good life with one's family and in society

The *most fundamental purpose* of working to make money is to be able to afford the goods and services needed to take care of people's most fundamental human concerns to:

1. ***Survive*** from moment to moment.

2. ***Adapt*** as our bodies and situations change.

3. ***Live a good life*** with one's spouse and children that is deeply meaningful, satisfying (no regrets), worthwhile and enjoyable,

   > … and to live with dignity in society with one's extended family, friends and neighbors,

   > … *including 25+ years of old age.*

The minimum amount businesspeople must earn and save during their career, according to economists, psychologists, scientists and philosophers, *is enough to afford the non-discretionary goods and services* everyone requires to survive day-to-day and adapt over time as people's bodies and circumstances change until they are at least 90 years old.

There are four **"non-discretionary goods and services"**, *according to economists.*

Non-discretionary means people *must* buy them, because if they are not available in sufficient quantities and quality human beings cannot survive in the moment or adapt over time as they and their situations change.

When human beings are unable to take satisfactory care of their non-discretionary concerns they and their spouse become desperate, stressed and unhealthy, and cannot live a good life.

The **four non-discretionary goods and services** *are:*

1. *Food*	Grocery stores	
2. *Housing*	Utilities, taxes, insurance, mortgage, maintenance, long-term upkeep	
3. *Medical Care*	Insurance, co-pays, out of pocket, pharmacies, doctors, medicine	
4. *Transportation*	Gas, insurance, service, tires, loan, long-term upkeep	

The amount of money businesspeople need to earn in order to save enough money by age 60 to live a good life for 25+ years of old age is surprisingly simple and easy to calculate.

Businesspeople already have records to determine how much food, housing, medical care and transportation cost them today. It's easy to adjust these costs, approximately, for old age to determine how much income they'll need to retire.

Every $40k of annual before-tax income businesspeople need to afford food, housing, medical care and transportation for 25+ years of old age requires them to have $1m saved and invested passively by age 60. ($40k is 4% of $1m.)

Every $100k of income, for example, businesspeople need when they retire with their spouse requires them to have $2.5m saved and invested.

Because of inflation, which averages 3% annually, the amount of money businesspeople and their spouse need to save to produce $100k in annual income increases by:

50% for *46-year-olds to $3.75m*

100% for *36-year-olds to $5m*

Decades of financial reports from private and public sources agree: businesspeople who continue to earn normal IR#3 Incomes *can't* make enough money to avoid running out of it with their spouse during old age.

When businesspeople decline or fail to earn *and* save enough money to afford the goods and services every human being requires, the situations they create as they age trigger increasing hardships, chronic financial stresses, desperation and despair.

These stresses are unhealthy. They make people ill, shorten their lifespans by as much as 20 years and make it impossible to live a good life.

Using Aji, *The Aji Source Fundamental Strategy* and the four fundamental tactics -- how to design an (1) offer, (2) practice, (3) narrative and (4) strategy -- enables businesspeople, and entire business organizations, to double their productivity, value and incomes so they can fulfill their life, financial and business ambitions to live a good life.

#2 - Formulate Philosophies of Care and Competition

Every industrial revolution creates new financial and competitive pressures that make it impossible to earn a living using old, or "traditional", business knowledge. Eventually, financial pressures and the suffering they cause to businesspeople and their families force them to create or adopt a new philosophical approach to why and how to make money.

Those who resist adapting and changing how they think and act to make money suffer and fail to make "enough money" to take care of their family until they surrender, learn and adapt.

Since most businesspeople are not yet able to earn and save "enough money" when 25+ years of old age is included, and will discover they can double their incomes when they use Aji, it is clear they need to learn how to adapt and quit using IR#3 business skills.

*****

To use computers and the internet competitively to produce a Normal IR#4 Income that is twice as high as the Normal IR#3 Income most businesspeople continue to earn,

... businesspeople need new:

1. *Orientations*

2. *Intentions*

3. *Business skills*

The first two sets of new orientations, intentions and skills that businesspeople use to double their productivity, value and incomes -- their *Philosophies of Care and Competition* -- are philosophical, or thoughtful. Together, the two new philosophies shift businesspeople's orientations from task orientation to strategic orientation.

The first set, their ***Philosophies of Care***, is an interpretation of the completely new *business concerns* individuals and businesses need to take care of using their computers and the internet, and in what sequence, to double their incomes.

* Aji shows businesspeople how to take care of 22 fundamental business concerns.

    Read about the *Fundamental Business Concerns* on aji.com, ASAP.

    Read the list of *fundamental business, career, human and marriage* in these notes.

The second set, ***Philosophies of Competition***, is an interpretation of the completely new *competitive situations, capabilities and strategies* that have appeared in IR#4, and how to compete in them successfully enough to double one's income.

IR#4 is the most:

1. Rapidly changing

2. Intensely competitive

3. Increasingly complex

4. Technologically advanced global marketplace in history

In IR#4, new competitive situations are created throughout the day. None are obvious, objective, perceivable or commonsensical. No one can "figure them out".

Each one needs to be approached, and interpreted, using a competitive, fundamental strategy such as Aji.

When businesspeople use Aji, for instance, they learn to interpret each IR#4 competitive situation as a new set of:

1. *Competitive threats* they must avoid, or cope with

2. *Competitive obligations* they must fulfill to:

    Keep their existing opportunities to make money

    Produce new opportunities to make money

    Avoid avoidable threats, risks and costs

3. *Competitive opportunities* they need to exploit

    ... to fulfill their financial, career and business intentions.

This part of The Strategy reveals why and how "traditional" IR#3 orientations, intentions and business skills such as hard work, reliance on common sense and task orientation are not competitive in IR#4.

Philosophies of Competition show why knowing how to:

1. *Learn competitively* to increase their competitive capabilities and advantages, productivity, value and incomes

2. *Communicate* ambitions, moods, explanations (DMRVPs), distinctions, interpretations, intentions, commitments, practices and outcomes, completely, strategically and competitively

3. *Coordinate* thought and action using commitments, e.g., requests, assessments, assertions, promises, declarations, complaints, apologies, offers, etc.

4. *Design and execute* steady streams of fresh, new offers, practices, narratives and strategies

    … is the only way to compete successfully in rapidly changing and complex competitive situations

    … when using computers and the internet

    … to earn and save enough money to live a good life when 25+ years of old age with one's spouse is included.

#3 - Learn tactical, strategic and competitive knowledge

All three categories of knowledge -- tactical, strategic and competitive -- are needed to execute The Strategy and double productivity, value and incomes.

All three are significantly more powerful ways of thinking and acting with one's computer and the internet to make money than using common sense to get jobs done.

Each one enables businesspeople to design and execute fresh, new offers, practices, narratives and strategies (OPNS), to execute The Strategy, and to double productivity, value and income.

What does "knowledge" mean when using Aji?

Knowledge is *the capability to produce an outcome intentionally in a given set of circumstances*, such as knowing how to hire an employee, speak a compelling business narrative or sell a service to make money.

Whenever a new competitive situation appears, such as a new tool or application, or a new offer made by a competitor, which can happen as often as every 15 minutes in IR#4,

> … businesspeople need to be willing and able to design their own new knowledge in the form of being able to produce new and more valuable outcomes with OPNS in as little as 15 minutes, too.

With Aji, learning, or accumulating knowledge to produce new competitive outcomes as competitive situations change, is done all day, every day.

> *Being in an Aji IFP is one of the new competitive practices IR#4 businesspeople use to steadily increase their competitive capabilities and advantages, productivity, value and incomes to fulfill their financial, career and business intentions.*

Tactical knowledge, such as how to design a new offer,

> … is used to change competitive situations, or their threats, obligations and opportunities,

> … such as to produce new customers, employees, employers, colleagues and vendors,

> … to advance action, or make progress, executing a strategy or larger plan of action.

Examples of tactical knowledge include designing new OPNS, selling, leading a meeting and showing someone how to design a new business narrative to advance action, or make progress, to produce a strategy's objective.

Strategic knowledge is used to:

1. *Execute* a strategy

   … e.g., knowing how to use a sequence of tactics to produce a sequence of interim situations to make progress, or advance action, to produce a strategic objective.

2. *Improve* the execution of a strategy

   … e.g., knowing how to reduce an action plan's costs (time, energy, money and lost opportunities).

3. *Make a new strategy* possible

   … e.g., knowing how to design and execute a new strategy.

Knowing how to design a fresh, new business practice that improves how you execute *The Aji Source Fundamental Strategy*, or fulfill one of its 12 intentions, is strategic knowledge in IR#4 when using computers and the internet.

Competitive knowledge is ***competitive capabilities***,

> ... such as superior identities of one's trustworthiness, value, authority, leadership and dignity,

> ... and knowing how to design OPNS with marginal utilities that make them fresh, new, highly valued and scarce relative to demand,

> ... that are used to create and maintain *competitive advantages* that double productivity, value and incomes every day.

#4 - Use Ethics of Power

"Ethics" are standards of conduct based in a standard of values, e.g., moral, safety, financial and medical ethics that enable people to live a good life.

"Ethics of Power" are ways of thinking and acting in the marketplace, or in IR#4's competitive situations, that increase businesspeople's competitive capabilities and advantages.

Aji uses about 50 different Ethics of Power, which you can find in *Aji, An IR#4 Business Philosophy*, such as:

1. Use new Aji dominant strategies, i.e., a competitive, fundamental strategy and four tactics.

2. Design and execute offers whose *marginal utilities* are highly valued and scarce.

3. *Learn competitively* all day using recursion, recurrence and reciprocation.

4. *Always move first, fast and persistently* to produce steady streams of OPNS needed to make money in competitive situations, instead of thinking about it or waiting to feel comfortable.

5. Establish identities of *superior* trustworthiness, value, authority, leadership and dignity with business narratives.

6. Build IR#4 Networks of Capabilities.

7. Lead, manage and govern one's career and business, always (personal responsibility).

IR#3's ethics of power, or those invented before 1980 that worked with single-purpose tools, or before computers were first sold, such as "working hard" while relying on common sense to complete tasks and make incremental improvements by executing processes and procedures, *are now common, inferior strategically, uncompetitive and define mediocre outcomes in IR#4.*

IR#4 Ethics of Power are tactical, strategic and competitive, and always increase *competitive capabilities and advantages.*

#5 - Design new offers, practices, narratives and strategies (OPNS)

This is Aji's "tactical pivot".

A new dominant strategy

A new action package for IR#4

This is where new OPNS are first designed and used to make money tactically and strategically to execute The Strategy.

A *"tactic"* is an action, or practice, that is used to change a situation to advance action, or make progress, needed to execute a strategy, or produce a "strategic objective".

A *"tactical pivot"* is the set of actions, or practices, people need to know to execute a strategy, e.g., drive a car, sell a service, lead a meeting or build a house.

Using new tools competitively to make money, i.e., computers and the internet, requires businesspeople and entire businesses to learn and use a new:

1. Tactical pivot

2. Dominant strategy

3. Action package

Once businesspeople learn each of Aji's four fundamental tactics, they can begin to execute The Strategy, lead an Aji IFP, and start to double their productivity, value and incomes.

The four most fundamental practices businesspeople and businesses perform tactically to make money in the marketplace are designing their own steady streams of (1) offers, (2) practices, (3) narratives and (4) strategies, or OPNS.

These include goods and services, of course, as well as every thought and action that is invented, learned and used to produce them.

The more OPNS businesspeople and businesses design and execute strategically and competitively, the more likely they are to fulfill their financial, career and business intentions.

This makes knowing how to design and execute steady streams of OPNS that are (1) fresh, (2) new, (3) highly valued and (4) scarce relative to demand with customers, employees, employers, colleagues and vendors,

… an Ethic of Power or a source of "good aji" in IR#4.

Designing new OPNS is an Ethic of Power because it forces, seduces or compels Buyers to:

1. ***Accept offers quickly*** to produce the *lowest possible transaction costs*

2. ***Increase their willingness to pay a premium*** to produce the *highest possible purchase price*

"Offers" are announcements we make to people that we would like to transact with them, or exchange goods and services for a purchase price.

When people transact and their capabilities to take care of their families are increased because they ***"made money"***, they have made a ***"profit"***.

It is in the moment that two parties agree to transact that money is made for each party.

"Practices" are named actions people use to:

1. Take care of *concerns*

2. Cope with *situations*

3. Increase their *capabilities* to produce outcomes to fulfill their intentions

4. Design and execute *strategies*, or create ways to produce outcomes, that people name in order to identify them.

(CSCS)

"Business narratives" are always action stories about making and fulfilling commitments to make money needed to survive, adapt and live a good life.

They must always be complete (no parts can be missing, ever) because that is required to make them effective, strategic and competitive.

Each must contain a complete (1) exposition, (2) conflict, (3) rising action, (4) resolution and (5) denouement.

* *Making money is always really about the denouement.*

"Strategies" are complex action plans executed to produce an intended outcome, or "strategic objective".

Strategies are always constituted and organized the same way, fundamentally.

They always contain:

1. *Commitments to produce an outcome* that is called a strategic objective by performing…

2. A *sequence of tactics* to produce…

3. A *sequence of situations*…

> … that progress, or advance the action,

> … *until the purpose of the strategy is fulfilled.*

Walking up a flight of stairs is a simple example of a strategy, or action plan, with an objective, tactics and interim situations.

1. Getting to the top of the stairs is the *strategic objective.*

2. Stepping up with one's right and left foot, and repeating the actions, is the *sequence of tactics.*

3. Each step up the stairs produces the *sequence of new situations* that makes it possible to advance action to step up to the next one

> … until the *strategic objective* is produced.

A sales conversation is a complex example.

Each part of the conversation -- marketing, prospecting, greeting, qualifying, presenting, objections, closing, re-closing, fulfilling and satisfying -- is its own mini-strategy with its own objective, tactics and situations.

To produce a transaction and "make money", which is the Sales Conversation's *strategic objective*,

> ... businesspeople use a *sequence of tactics* such as Greeting and Qualifying Questions

> ... to produce a *sequence of situations* with the Buyer (new interpretations and commitments) such as them trusting and accepting the offer,

> ... which is the *strategic objective*.

#6 - Build IR#4 Tactical, Strategic and Competitive Networks of Capabilities (IR#4 NWC)

This is Aji's "strategic pivot".

A new Dominant Strategy

A New Action Package for IR#4

This is where the strategic capability to design *and* execute action plans to produce competitive capabilities and advantages needed to double productivity, value and incomes is made.

Simply put, until businesspeople are able to perform Aji's four fundamental tactics (Part #5 of The Strategy) and are able to design and execute their own offers, practices, narratives and strategies (OPNS), they cannot execute Parts #6 - #12 of The Strategy.

* It takes most businesspeople about 100 days to complete the first half of *The Aji Starter's Course* on aji.com to learn the four tactics.

Once businesspeople learn the four fundamental tactics -- how to design and execute OPNS -- *they can build a completely new "Source of Strategic Power"* -- IR#4 Networks of Capabilities (IR#4 NWC) -- *to double their productivity, value and incomes.*

IR#4 NWC could not exist practically, or technically, before computers and the internet made remote learning, communication, coordination and production possible.

When using Aji, businesspeople build an array of IR#4 NWC such as networks of transaction, tactical support and collegial help to increase their productivity and value.

The purpose of IR#4 NWC is to increase businesspeople's autonomies, or freedom, to produce highly valued accomplishments, or Parts #7 and #8 of The Strategy.

IR#4's Networks of Tactical, Strategic and Competitive Capabilities are global, strategic and competitive. They are not local, except by coincidence.

IR#4's Networks of *Capabilities* replace reliance on IR#3 networks of *convenience*,

> … which are local, cheap, commonsensical, task-oriented,

> … and a source of uncompetitive ambitions, moods, explanations, distinctions, interpretations, intentions, commitments, practices and outcomes,

> … when using computers and the internet to make money.

As businesspeople increase their capabilities to design and execute their own OPNS (Part #5),

> … and begin to build their strategic and competitive capabilities and advantages with IR#4 Networks of *Capabilities* (Part #6),

> … their productivity, value and incomes increase naturally.

#7 - *Increase autonomies, competitive capabilities and advantages*

To double businesspeople's productivity, value and incomes, or the enterprise value of a business,

> … people and organizations *must* increase their freedoms, competitive capabilities (skills) and competitive advantages (marginal utilities),

> … to *learn, communicate, coordinate* new thought and action, and *design* and execute fresh, new offers, practices, narratives and strategies (OPNS).

Businesspeople *can't* be "too busy" to learn in IR#4 because they are working hard with their common sense to get the job done.

> In IR#3 being too busy to learn was a virtue. It meant workers already knew what to do and how to do it to get their jobs done so resources needed to "train" them were not needed.

Business is a game of power. It's about producing capabilities to produce outcomes (OPNS) that are superior to one's competitors in the eyes of Buyers, i.e., customers, employers, employees, colleagues and vendors.

> Whoever has the most power to produce superior outcomes wins and makes the most money.

Knowledge is power needed to produce and increase competitive capabilities and advantages in IR#4.

> In *non-competitive* situations, knowledge is the capability to produce an outcome intentionally in a given set of circumstances, such as growing a garden, driving to the store or changing a diaper.

> In *competitive situations* such as designing an offer or running a race, power is the capability to produce a superior outcome in the eyes of the judges, or Buyers.

The monopolies and auctions superior OPNS produce naturally and spontaneously compel Buyers -- customers, employees, employers, colleagues and vendors -- to:

> *1. **Buy quickly*** to produce the *lowest possible transaction costs*

> *2. **Increase their willingness to pay a premium*** to produce the *highest possible purchase price*

Knowledge is also freedom, or the *absence* of unwanted constraints and limitations on a human being's abilities to think and act to fulfill their intentions.

> The more knowledge businesspeople acquire, the more power and freedom they have to fulfill their financial, career and business intentions, or to become rich.

Ignorance and working without a network, on the other hand, reduces and suppresses the freedom businesspeople must have to think and act as they need to in order to fulfill their financial, career and business intentions.

One way to acquire new tactical, strategic and competitive knowledge, power and freedom, is to learn Aji, or how to execute *The Aji Source Fundamental Strategy* throughout the day, instead of using hard work, common sense and task orientation, which shut down power in IR#4.

Another way IR#4 businesspeople who know Aji increase their knowledge, power and freedom is by building their IR#4 Networks of Capabilities (Part #6) and working with them in an Aji IFP.

Businesspeople increase their autonomies, power and freedom to make money as they increase their abilities to think and act tactically, strategically and competitively to produce steady streams of highly valued accomplishments and build superior identities of trustworthiness, value, authority, leadership and dignity.

When businesspeople use their IR#4 NWC to increase their competitive capabilities to (1) design a new *offer,* (2) execute a new *practice,* (3) speak a new *business narrative* or (4) plan a new *strategy* to execute *The Aji Source Fundamental Strategy*,

... they increase their autonomy, or freedom, to fulfill their financial, career and business intentions.

* * * * *

#8 - *Produce highly valued and scarce accomplishments*

The marketplace understands the dangers of bullshit, hype, humbug, lies, glamour and caveat emptor (buyer beware) quite well. The idea of "fake it 'til you make it" is deeply flawed.

To double productivity, value and incomes, ***"proof of knowledge"*** as well as identities of *superior* (1) trustworthiness, (2) value, (3) authority, (4) leadership and (5) dignity (TVAL&D) are always required.

The only ***proof of knowledge*** and expertise that Buyers will accept, or of people's claims that they can produce an outcome in a given set of circumstances, is their history of ***accomplishments.***

Everything else is simply talk. It's noise people make.

To produce the proof, businesspeople must be able to explain how their accomplishments *are proof* of their knowledge with seductive and compelling explanations using (1) descriptions, (2) meanings, (3) relevance, (4) value and (5) purposes, or DMRVP.

In addition to proving businesspeople have the capabilities to produce an outcome they claim is highly valued, accomplishments prove *superior* TVAL&D.

It doesn't matter whether we are talking about answering simple questions for customers or building a football stadium.

To produce *any* outcome intentionally:

People must be *trustworthy* enough to produce it.

They must know what is, and is not, important, useful and worthwhile. (*Value)*

They must know what is, and is not, required, forbidden and allowed to produce an outcome intentionally in a given set of circumstances. (*Authority*)

They must know how to anticipate and have others accept their help to deal with new threats, obligations and opportunities that exist in the situations they encounter by having their "leadership offers" accepted. (*Leadership*)

And, they must act with integrity and have value with those around them at work and in their family and communities. (*Dignity*)

Therefore, the more sincere, reliable and expert businesspeople become as they execute The Strategy to produce their own steady streams of accomplishments that are fresh, new, highly valued and scarce relative to demand -- regardless of their role in business -- the more evidence or grounding they produce to support claims that their trustworthiness, value, authority, leadership and dignity is *superior* to their competitors.

#9 - *Establish identities of* superior *trustworthiness, value, authority, leadership and dignity (TVAL&D)*

Business is social. Being a distrustful and prideful lone ranger who will not learn, accept new interpretations or trust others, shuts down the competitive capabilities and advantages businesspeople need in IR#4 to double their incomes.

People's willingness to transact with a Seller depends upon the Seller's identities of TVAL&D. This is because people and their careers, businesses and families are fragile. They are easily harmed or ruined when betrayed. It doesn't matter whether the betrayal is intentional, accidental or due to incompetence.

Identities are characterizations, or interpretations, of a person's or business' virtues or capabilities to fulfill their commitments, or to produce intended outcomes in a given set of circumstances such as rapidly changing and intensely competitive situations.

They are interpretations that characterize a Seller's virtues and vices, such as their trustworthiness or mediocrity.

They help Buyers anticipate how Sellers will think and act to fulfill their commitments with OPNS, including goods and services, to help Buyers fulfill their intentions.

A businessperson's identities, or characterizations, about their TVAL&D enable customers, employers, employees, colleagues, vendors and competitors to judge the likely costs, risks and returns of accepting an offer, practice, narrative or strategy from them.

The most important and fundamental characterizations businesspeople must work to produce to double their productivity, value and incomes are that their TVAL&D are *satisfactory* and *superior* to competitors'.

The more rewarding, scarce, inexpensive and low risk businesspeople and businesses make it to accept their offers, practices, narratives or strategies,

> ... the easier it is for Buyers to produce a return and the more profitable, valuable and competitive the offer becomes.

The more businesspeople's identities of TVAL&D are *superior* to those of competitors because of the outcomes they can produce expertly and reliably (and it doesn't matter what role they hold),

> ... the more they can produce monopolies and auctions naturally and spontaneously for their goods and services to drive up their incomes or revenues

> ... or the enterprise value of their business.

#10 - Hold highly compensated leadership roles

One of the new competitive situations produced by the most rapidly changing, competitive, complex and technologically advanced global marketplaces in history creates every day, all day,

> … that characterizes IR#4,

> … is an explosion in the need for businesspeople who are able to lead others in meetings, when managing or when selling,

> *… who actually know what they are doing when they lead or follow.*

What businesspeople do when they learn how to lead from Aji is design OPNS, or a Leadership Offer, to help others fulfill their intentions to produce outcomes in competitive situations that the leader understands better than their followers.

In return for their leadership, *followers agree to:*

1. *Accept the leader's interpretations* of threats to avoid, obligations to fulfill and opportunities to exploit.

2. *Fulfill the leader's requests to coordinate thought and action* with other followers, employees or colleagues to produce outcomes.

The explosion in the need for leaders in IR#4 is a consequence of how IR#4's competitive situations change throughout the day, especially changes in standards of value -- what is most important, useful and worthwhile.

This means someone working in a warehouse who is using a new application will inevitably find themselves in meetings where they understand the competitive threats, obligations and opportunities the application brings into existence for the business better than their colleagues, employees or employers.

In IR#4, every business owner, executive, manager, supervisor, salesperson and individual contributor must know, formally, how to lead people through competitive situations.

Businesspeople lead by offering helpful interpretations about how to cope with and exploit a new situation's threats, obligations and opportunities that they are in a better position to understand than those around them.

They lead by explaining the new specific threats, obligations and opportunities in a competitive situation, or with a new device or competitor, so that their followers, including their managers, are able to think and act effectively in the situation to fulfill their intentions.

To lead, businesspeople need to be able to speak descriptions, meanings, relevance, value and purposes (DMRVP) about a situation's threats, obligations and opportunities, so that they are (1) easy, (2) enjoyable and (3) definitive to hear.

#11 - *Build strategic and competitive business organizations*

Business organizations are groups of businesspeople whose *orientations, intentions, commitments and skills* are arranged, or organized, around the fulfillment of a shared intention to make money by thinking, acting and working together.

The strategic and competitive purpose of building business organizations is two-fold:

> *First,* to increase the power of businesspeople's *leadership roles* with their followers and in the marketplace.

> *Second,* to exploit the organization's *capital structures,*

>> ... i.e., (1) human capital,(2) capital equipment, (3) capital inventories of OPNS, (4) operating capital and (5) financial capital.

To compete successfully in rapid change, increasing complexity, intense competition and advancing technologies,

> ... a business organization's orientations, intentions to produce outcomes and business skills,

> ... need to be *ambitious, thoughtful, tactical, strategic and competitive,*

> ... and not task-oriented or commonsensical.

The organization's competitive capabilities using the first 10 parts of The Strategy need to be solid.

That is, the businesspeople who constitute the organization, or who coordinate thought and action together to produce outcomes to fulfill the business' mission, must first be able to:

Part #1 - Constitute their real and deeply meaningful financial, career and business *ambitions*

Part #2 - Use *Philosophies of Care and Competition* that exploit the new tactical, strategic and competitive capabilities computers and the internet make possible

Part #3 - Learn Aji's *Tactical, Strategic and Competitive Knowledge*, instead of using common sense

Part #4 - Formulate and use *Ethics of Power*, instead of being busy and working hard with common sense

Part #5 - *Produce offers, practices, narratives and strategies* that are fresh, new, highly valued and scarce relative to demand that they can use to execute The Strategy in as little as 15 minutes, instead of getting jobs done

Part #6 - *Build IR#4 Networks of Capabilities* (customers, employees, colleagues, etc., whose ambitions and knowledge are strategic), instead of using IR#3's networks of convenience because they are cheap, obvious and local

Part #7 - Increase *autonomies* continuously by working with IR#4 Networks of Capabilities to reduce unwanted limitations and constraints to produce highly valued accomplishments,

> … instead of being "too busy" working hard with common sense to learn, communicate, coordinate and design

Part #8 - Produce *highly valued and scarce accomplishments* every day, instead of making incremental improvements that don't really matter

Part #9 - *Establish identities* of *superior* trustworthiness, value, authority, leadership and dignity with customers, employers, employees, colleagues and vendors,

> … instead of faking it, being arrogant and prideful, or bullshitting

Part #10 - Hold *highly compensated leadership roles* in the marketplace with followers who accept their interpretations about competitive situations and fulfill their requests to coordinate thought and action,

... instead of common and low-paid ones

Then the focus on the business organization's competitiveness shifts to using Ethics of Power that continually increase the business':

Competitive capabilities	The *skills*, actions and practices businesspeople will use to produce competitive advantages, such as how to design a business narrative or lead in a meeting
Competitive advantages	The *marginal utilities* of every OPNS used to produce goods and services that make their benefits superior to those produced by competitors

#12 - *Anticipate future competitive situations*

Anticipating new competitive situations -- their *threats, obligations and opportunities* -- is essential in rapid change.

The skill to anticipate new competitive situations increases the amount of *time* businesspeople and businesses have to design fresh, new offers, practices, narratives and strategies (OPNS) needed to increase their competitive capabilities and advantages, or their value in the marketplace.

The more time employees, employers, vendors, colleagues and customers have to design fresh, new OPNS, especially their goods and services,

   ... the more likely they are to create and maintain
   monopolies *and* ***auctions*** *by:*

   1. Being ***first to market*** with their OPNS

   2. Having the ***best designed OPNS*** with the most valuable marginal utilities

   3. Having the ***most complex and powerful combination*** of new technologies or tools

Time is the first space of possibilities that limits and shapes businesspeople's thoughts and actions to fulfill their financial intentions.

The more time businesspeople have to design and execute fresh, new OPNS because they are able to anticipate competitive situations, the more likely they are to fulfill their financial, career and business intentions.

When there is no time because a competitor's new offer is already launched, thought and action to take market share with competitive advantages, or to fulfill financial, career and business intentions, is no longer possible.

When individuals or businesses create a *monopoly* with their OPNS by being (1) first to market, (2) the best designed or (3) the most powerful combination of new technologies,

... they produce *auctions* that drive up their value, incomes and revenues.

Producing *monopolies* and *auctions* with fresh, new OPNS for employers, employees, customers, colleagues and vendors compels or seduces Buyers to:

1. *Accept offers quickly*, which produces the *lowest possible transaction costs*

2. *Increase their willingness to pay a premium,* which produces the *highest possible purchase price, or compensation*

The "Aji Action Package"

Ambitions, Moods, Explanations

Distinctions, Interpretations, Intentions

Commitments, Practices, Outcomes

What Is an "Action Package"?

Aji Action Package Distinctions

Actions and Skills Exist in Businesspeople's Language

Philosophy of Competition, Part #2 of The Strategy

IR#4 Orientations, Intentions and Skills

8 Fundamental Action Distinctions Flow in Sequence

Notice

Observe

Assess

Design

Craft

Speak

Prepare to Act

Act

What Is an "Action Package"?

An *"action package"* is a set of nine linguistic actions businesspeople and businesses use when they think and act to make money, or to fulfill their financial, career and business intentions.

When businesspeople use a traditional IR#3 action package that is task-oriented and relies on common sense, they produce a Normal IR#3 Income that is far too low to enable them to raise their family and save enough to afford 25+ years of old age with their spouse.

When businesspeople use *Aji's Action Package*, which is strategic and competitive, they can produce a Normal IR#4 Income that is twice as high. This helps them save enough money to avoid running out of it with their spouse when they retire.

One way to speak about how businesspeople think and act to earn a living is to describe what they are doing with their bodies, how fast they are moving or where they move.

This method was used in IR#3, which ended in the 1980s.

It works when businesspeople use single-purpose tools in sequence to perform repetitive processes and procedures while making incremental improvements.

Another way to observe how businesspeople are thinking and acting to produce competitive outcomes *that is at least twice as effective* is to describe the action package they use when they think, speak commitments and act.

This method, which is part of The Strategy's tactical, strategic and competitive knowledge (Part #3), enables businesspeople and businesses in IR#4 to:

1. Exploit the new tactical, strategic and *competitive capabilities and advantages* computers and the internet make possible.

2. Design their own *offers, practices, narratives and strategies* (OPNS) to increase their productivity, value and incomes.

3. Build *IR#4 Networks of Capabilities* to increase their competitive capabilities and advantages.

4. Increase their *autonomies*, or freedom, competitive capabilities and competitive advantages, to fulfill their financial, career and business intentions.

5. Produce steady streams of *highly valued accomplishments* that are scarce relative to demand.

6. Build *superior identities* of trustworthiness, value, authority, leadership and dignity.

7. Hold *highly compensated leadership roles.*

8. Build strategic and competitive *business organizations.*

9. *Anticipate* new competitive threats to avoid, obligations to fulfill and opportunities to exploit.

Businesspeople's action package is the language they use to think, make assessments, design new intentions, make commitments, and speak and act in the marketplace.

It's how they speak to themselves and others.

It's what determines how they speak their offers and act to fulfill them in the marketplace to make money.

It gives rise to what the rest of us hear them say and see them do to produce accomplishments and the income they earn.

In other words,

… it's businesspeople's action package that is creating the offers, practices, narratives and strategies we hear and see in the marketplace,

… and not how we see their bodies move.

When businesspeople change their action package, or the language they are using to think and act when they make money, so that it is strategic and competitive, rather than task-oriented,

… their productivity, value and incomes can double.

* * * * *

Human language includes how human beings think, learn, communicate, coordinate thought and action, and act individually and in networks to produce important outcomes to:

#1 - Take care of their *concerns*

#2 - Cope with *situations* in which they find themselves

#3 - Increase their *capabilities* to compete successfully

#4 - Design and execute new *strategies*, or new ways to use their computers, the internet and Aji

(CSCS)

… to produce outcomes that fulfill their intentions.

When businesspeople, or business organizations, use Aji's Action Package, they begin to think and act ambitiously, thoughtfully, strategically and competitively,

… and quit using their common sense to work hard completing tasks.

The action package invented in IR#3 that enabled businesspeople to earn a living while using single-purpose tools such as hammers, typewriters and landline telephones,

> *... suppresses businesspeople's incomes by at least 100% when they use computers and the internet.*

The Aji Action Package included with *The Aji Source Fundamental Strategy* that is used to execute it:

Frees businesspeople up to use their computers and the internet in ways IR#3's action package cannot.

Enables businesspeople to use their computers and the internet tactically, strategically and competitively, and to quit being task-oriented and commonsensical.

Shows them how to increase their productivity, value and incomes, and why using The Strategy works so that they can see it for themselves.

The Aji Action Package

Actions and Skills Exist in Businesspeople's Language

To increase businesspeople's productivity, value and incomes, they need to change the *language, concepts, practices* and *outcomes* they use to make money, or to earn and save enough money, to live a good life with their spouse until they are at least 90 years old.

They need to change their action package, or their:

1. *Ambitions*
2. *Moods*
3. *Explanations*
4. *Distinctions*
5. *Interpretations*
6. *Intentions*
7. *Commitments*
8. *Practices*
9. *Outcomes*

The Aji Action Package is a list of the different categories of linguistic actions businesspeople use when they think and act to produce outcomes that fulfill their financial, career and business intentions.

They are different forms of commitments and actions, e.g., promises, requests, declarations, assessments, assertions, offers, practices, narratives, strategies, etc.

Every human being's action package is fundamentally the same. They always contain the same fundamental nine linguistic actions or ways people think, act and speak to themselves and others.

People's action packages differ specifically depending upon (1) the combination of fundamental and specific outcomes they intend to produce, and (2) the threats, obligations and opportunities in which they must think and act to produce them.

> CEOs and salespeople have different action packages, for instance, because the outcomes they intend to produce are different *fundamentally*.

> Salespeople who sell farm equipment will have action packages that are different *specifically* than those who sell legal services. The outcomes they intend to produce are *specifically* different even though selling, or producing a transaction, is always the same *fundamentally*.

Simply put, businesspeople who earn high incomes use a different action package than those who earn low ones.

> It's easy to hear when they speak.

> They have different ambitions, moods, explanations, distinctions, interpretations, intentions, commitments, practices and outcomes.

Aji's Action Package enables businesspeople to exploit the new tactical, strategic and competitive capabilities brought into existence by computers and the internet.

It is *specifically* different from the action package invented before 1980 that most businesspeople continue to use that enables them to exploit the task-fulfilling capabilities produced by single-purpose tools.

Using Aji and executing *The Aji Source Fundamental Strategy*, all day, every day, changes businesspeople's orientation, intentions and skills in all nine categories of the Action Package. It changes them from IR#3's task orientation, incremental improvements and reliance on common sense, which is a *specific* set of words, concepts and practices, to using their computers strategically and competitively instead,

> … which is a *different specific set* of words, concepts and practices.

Aji's Action Package enables businesspeople to increase their competitive capabilities and advantages so that they can *double* their productivity, value and incomes.

When Aji's Action Package is used by a business organization's employers and employees, they can *double* the enterprise's value.

Put another way:

To succeed in IR#3 and earn a Normal IR#3 Income

>   *… required businesspeople to learn and use a different action package*

>   *… than the one businesspeople need to learn and use in IR#4 when using their computers and the internet*

>   *… to earn a Normal IR#4 Income that is twice as high.*

Aji Action Package Distinctions

When Businesspeople Use Aji's Action Package,

They Start to Earn a Normal IR#4 Income That Is Twice as High

As a Normal IR#3 Income

Ambitions   Personal intentions to produce outcomes that are deeply meaningful, satisfying, worthwhile and enjoyable in the future, such as earning enough money during one's career to avoid running out of it with one's spouse, ever

Moods   Narratives about future possibilities to succeed or live a good life, accompanied by body sensations, e.g., passion vs. indifference, humility vs. arrogance, ambition vs. reacting in the moment

Explanations   Claims and interpretations people accept using descriptions, meanings, relevance, value and purposes (DMRVP) about people, money, how people make money, how the marketplace works, etc., that shape how they think and act in the marketplace

*****

Distinctions   Words and concepts used to differentiate, establish and focus language, thought and action so that people can fulfill their intentions to produce outcomes

Interpretations   Assessments and judgments people use to determine their situations' threats, obligations and opportunities, and to design and execute action to produce outcomes that fulfill their intentions

Intentions   Personal commitments and plans to produce outcomes

*****

Commitments   Declarations to colleagues, customers, employers, employees and vendors to be the cause of producing an outcome that fulfills, or is coherent with, their promises, requests, assessments and assertions

Practices   Named actions used to learn, communicate and coordinate thought and action, and to produce outcomes, e.g., leading, managing and selling

Outcomes   The results or situations produced by businesspeople's thoughts and actions, or their action package

Action Package Summary

Philosophy of Competition, Part #2 of The Strategy

IR#4 Orientations, Intentions and Skills

Action packages are, first, an expression of businesspeople's *"way of being" in the marketplace*. It is the way they are *oriented*.

Are they *being* ambitious and competitive, or apathetic and aimless (even though they work hard) about their financial situations when they retire?

Are they *being* task-oriented or strategically oriented?

Are they *being* tactical, strategic and competitive, or determined to get jobs done without concern for the savings they'll need for old age with their spouse?

Are they *being* serious, thoughtful, practical, humble, enthusiastic, passionate and dignified, or are they *being* casual, prideful, jerky, conceited, arrogant and indifferent?

* * * * *

Action packages include "dominant strategies".

Dominant strategies are the best course of action to take in competitive situations out of a dozen or more choices, regardless of what competitors do.

They are different in different competitive situations with different threats to avoid, obligations to fulfill and opportunities to exploit, and to produce different outcomes.

They produce "good aji".

The "old" dominant strategy for IR#3, which ended when personal computers and the internet began being sold, now defines mediocrity in IR#4.

IR#3's dominant strategy is to:

1. *Always work hard*

2. *Focus on getting jobs done*

3. *Rely on one's common sense*

4. *Use processes and procedures*

5. *Make incremental* improvements

Aji's new dominant strategy for IR#4 is to use a competitive, fundamental strategy with four equally fundamental tactics, rather than common sense, hard work and determination.

To succeed in IR#4 *using computers and the internet* and produce a Normal IR#4 Income that is twice as high as a Normal IR#3 Income,

> ... businesspeople must use a new Action Package that includes new IR#4 dominant strategies,

> ... or a completely new set of (1) *orientations,* (2) *intentions* and (3) *business skills.*

Orientations, Intentions, Skills and Tactics

Orientations are...

Ways of being, e.g., serious, humble, ambitious, eager, sincere, enthusiastic, strategic, competitive,

... or, cynical, distrustful, prideful, self-important, pretentious, entitled, aimless, flip, argumentative

Directions for thought and action, e.g., ambitious vs. aimless

Ways of relating, e.g., accepting the challenge vs. being resigned, or being enthusiastic and passionate, rather than passive, disinterested and cynical

Commitments and intentions, e.g.,

... good enough is good enough to get through the day

vs.

... producing steady streams of highly valued accomplishments with competitive capabilities and advantages

... that include taking care of one's most fundamental human concerns, such as having enough money to take care of one's spouse until they are 90 years old

Physical locations, positions or postures with regard to something else,

      … e.g., working with an IR#3 Network of Convenience, avoiding or engaging with an IR#4 Network of Capabilities online with colleagues and teachers

Predispositions   beliefs, attitudes, intentions, interpretations, assessments, wants, wishes, desires,

           … e.g., relying on common sense and popular culture for answers, knowledge and orientations, or being humble, ambitious and respecting knowledge

IR#3's orientation is to *be* task-oriented, commonsensical, process driven, satisfied with incremental improvements and hard working.

This group considers it a virtue that shows they are being productive and valuable when they are "too busy to learn".

IR#4's orientation is to *be* ambitious, strategic and competitive.

This group considers learning to increase their competitive capabilities and advantages, productivity, value and incomes, all day, every day, strategic, competitive and... *normal.*

Using Aji's Action Package makes everyday learning to fulfill their financial, career and business intentions... *easy, enjoyable and definitive.*

Intentions are...

The personal purposes, objectives or outcomes people mean or aim to produce with their thoughts and actions,

> ... e.g., increasing autonomies to double productivity, value and incomes.

Skills, or practices, are...

The named actions, or methods, people use to produce an outcome or fulfill their intentions,

> ... e.g., designing a new strategy or establishing superior identities of TVAL&D.

Tactics are ...

When a practice is used to produce a new situation that advances action to execute a strategy, which changes its orientation and intentions, it is called a "tactic",

> ... e.g., selling to make a transaction is a task but selling to execute a strategy to double one's income is a tactic.

8 Fundamental Action Distinctions

Flow in Sequence

(Language)

When working in rapidly changing and intensely competitive situations, businesspeople use the following action sequence all day, every day,

    … to declare their intentions, assess their competitive situations, design new offers, practices, narratives and strategies,

    … and use them to execute *The Aji Source Fundamental Strategy*.

1. ***Notice*** competitive situations exist, e.g., new competitive threats, obligations and opportunities.

2. ***Observe*** with distinctions the threats to avoid, obligations to fulfill and opportunities to exploit.

3. ***Assess*** the importance, utility and worth of a new competitive situation using competitive criteria and standards.

4. ***Design*** new intentions to produce outcomes, or a new strategic objective, e.g., double productivity, value and incomes.

5. ***Craft*** real properties so action is possible, e.g., commitments, tools, money, identities, plans, etc.

6. ***Speak*** intentions and commitments to produce outcomes to customers, employers, employees, colleagues and vendors.

7. ***Prepare*** to act with networks to produce new outcomes by inventing and learning newly designed practices.

8. ***Act*** to produce intended outcomes.

8 Fundamental Action Distinctions Flow in Sequence

Notice   *People* bring intentions, situations, concerns, capabilities and offers, practices, narratives and strategies (OPNS) into existence, or *become aware of something* such as a new tool or application, *by speaking about it to themselves or another.*

Observe   People *interpret* what they **notice** by using *tactical, strategic* and *competitive* distinctions -- facts and truths – to begin to discern the *threats* they may need to avoid, the *obligations* they may need to fulfill and the *opportunities* they may be able to exploit, such as:

1. How something appears to their *senses,* e.g., its color, size, smell, texture, sounds or taste

2. How it *operates*, e.g., it's very fast, works smoothly or saves energy

3. The *context* in which it exists, e.g., during the winter or in new competitive situations

4. How it makes people *feel psychologically* e.g., happy, comfortable, irritated, confident, ready to go -- that enable effective, strategic and competitive thought and action

Assess   People make *interpretations* about what they **observe** using criteria and standards to judge its important, utility and worth to help them produce outcomes that fulfill their intentions and commitments to:

Take care of human, career and business *concerns*

Produce satisfactory *situations* with threats, obligations and opportunities

Acquire new *capabilities* to think and act effectively

Execute *strategies*

Design   People use their **assessments** to declare *new intentions to produce outcomes,* commitments, concerns, situations, capabilities and strategies with their OPNS, which are called "new designs" to fulfill their intentions.

Craft   People give their **designs** for new OPNS "real properties" by making them specific and actionable to affect people's and businesses' concerns, situations, capabilities and strategies with commitments, networks, tools, money, identities, roles and organizations,

... to produce specific outcomes that fulfill specific intentions *so that action becomes possible.*

Speak   People make commitments, express their emotions, make judgments and explanations, produce action and transactions, or coordinate action for the sake of fulfilling intentions with their newly *crafted* OPNS.

When businesspeople design new OPNS to increase their competitive capabilities and advantages, productivity, value and incomes, they must speak them into existence for others.

Designing a new offer, practice, narrative and strategy, and even telling one's networks about them, doesn't mean they have a clue how to perform them.

Prepare   People learn, create, invent, design, plan action, assess,
to Act   deconstruct, anticipate, commit to produce outcomes that fulfill people's intentions,

… and practice, practice, practice newly designed thoughts, interpretations and actions to make and keep ever more valuable OPNS.

It's like learning to perform a new play from scratch.

First, it must be designed and crafted, or written.

Then the performers have to learn their lines and stage instructions.

And, finally, before they perform it for customers, they need to practice as many times as necessary to learn it.

Act   What people do, or not do, to produce an outcome to keep commitments, fulfill their intentions or to help another to:

1. Take care of a *concern*

2. Cope with a *situation*

3. Increase their *capabilities*

4. Produce or execute a *strategy*

*****

What Are Competitive Capabilities and Advantages?

Where Do Competitive Capabilities Come From?

Where Do Competitive Advantages Come From?

How do People Learn and Create Them?

What Is Knowledge?

Where Does Knowledge Come From?

What Are Competitive Capabilities and Advantages?

Before businesspeople can *double* their productivity, value and incomes, they *must* increase their:

Competitive capabilities	*Practices or skills* businesspeople have and can use to produce competitive advantages,
	… such as designing a new OPNS so that it is first to market, has a better design, or is more complex and useful,
	… to produce scarcity, monopolies and auctions, or provide a fresh, new capability or practice
Competitive advantages	*Outcomes, or marginal utilities,* produced with competitive capabilities whose marginal utilities are superior to, or more important, useful and worth buying than those produced by competitors

Before businesses or business organizations can increase their competitive capabilities and advantages, they have to learn:

1. What are competitive capabilities and advantages?

2. Where do they come from? (Sources of Power)

3. Why do they work with human beings or in the marketplace?

4. How do businesspeople produce, maintain and increase them?

5. How do businesspeople, and business organizations, use them:

   Tactically, to change situations to advance action, or make progress

   Strategically, to execute, improve or produce action plans

   Competitively, to produce outcomes superior in value compared to OPNS produced by competitors?

This is Part #3 of The Strategy: Tactical, strategic and competitive knowledge.

Where Do Competitive Capabilities and Advantages Come From?

How Do People Learn and Create Them?

What are competitive advantages?

They are offers, practices, narratives and strategies with marginal utilities that are superior to one's competitors. To be superior, their benefits or marginal utilities must be (1) *fresh,* (2) *new,* (3) *highly valued* and (4) *scarce relative to demand.*

An employee who can design new offers that increase revenues 20% more than any of their colleagues has a 20% marginal utility, a monopoly, they can use to produce auctions with employers to increase their incomes.

A business that can shorten production times by 20% relative to competitors has a 20% marginal utility, a monopoly, that will compel Buyers to:

1. ***Pay a premium*** (*highest possible purchase price*)

2. ***Accept offers quickly*** (*lowest possible transaction costs*)

… to gain the capability.

Where do competitive advantages come from?

They come from *competitive capabilities*, which are:

1. *Orientations,* such as being ambitious, tactical, strategic and competitive, and interested in accumulating power, instead of commonsensical, aimless, obvious, ordinary and mediocre

2. *Intentions* to produce outcomes that are strategic and competitive, rather than common,

   > … such as designing a new practice with highly valued marginal utilities,

   > … holding a leadership role,

   > … or establishing a superior identity, instead of getting a job done

3. *Business skills* to fulfill those intentions, such as how to:

   > … design a business narrative so it is seductive and compelling,

   > … increase the value of a strategy's objective,

   > … or halve the time needed to fulfill recurrent commitments, instead of using the usual cliches and metaphors about people's track records, etc., that are obvious, ordinary, typical… and uncompetitive.

Where do competitive capabilities come from?

They come from learning different forms of knowledge, or how to produce new outcomes that are highly valued and scarce such as knowing how to design offers, practices, narratives and strategies (OPNS) for every new competitive situation that appears.

It's knowing how to compete, or how to design and execute a competitive, fundamental strategy by designing steady streams of OPNS that:

Build an *IR#4 Network of Capabilities* that helps you to increase your competitive capabilities and advantages, productivity, value and income.

Increase your and other people's *autonomies, competitive capabilities and competitive advantages.*

Produce new *accomplishments* that are highly valued and scarce relative to demand.

Build *superior identities* about your trustworthiness, value, authority, leadership and dignity, to increase your value.

Hold *leadership roles* and produce followers who (1) accept your interpretations, (2) fulfill your requests and (3) increase your value.

Build a competitive *business organization.*

Anticipate threats to avoid, obligations to fulfill and opportunities to exploit in future competitive situations.

What Is Knowledge?

Knowledge is the capability to produce an intended outcome in a given set of circumstances.

To produce new and more competitive knowledge begins with declaring intentions to produce new outcomes in new competitive situations with new OPNS.

The knowledge is the capabilities businesspeople design and use to fulfill their new intentions, or to produce new outcomes tactically, strategically and competitively with new thought and action.

In IR#4, businesspeople use Aji to produce new knowledge, new OPNS, throughout the day, every day that they use to fulfill their financial, career and business intentions.

The rigid single-purpose tools businesspeople used in IR#3 prevented them from learning, or needing to learn, how to increase their value every day.

When new competitive situations produced with new OPNS appear rapidly in the marketplace, businesspeople must increase their knowledge to produce fresh, new OPNS to compete with them just as quickly.

Where does knowledge come from?

Knowledge is *linguistic interpretations* about how to think and act effectively to produce outcomes that fulfill people's intentions.

People *speak* knowledge into existence, which includes recording it or writing it down.

When people go to medical, engineering or law school, for instance, they listen/watch/read what their teachers say so they can "couple" with the language and become able to think and act with the DMRVP the teachers speak to produce their own OPNS.

Most language people learn is historical or cultural. As situations evolve in a society, or marketplace, politically or technologically, people invent new language with new *descriptions, meanings, relevance, value* and *purposes* (DMRVP) to cope with them.

When people learn how to become businesspeople during an industrial revolution, they are in danger of learning the wrong language about business. Instead of learning *new* ways to think and act in the new competitive situations industrial revolutions produce, which is always new language, or new DRMVPs, they continue to use linguistic distinctions and practices that have become common, obvious and easy to find but have been made obsolete and uncompetitive.

Consequently, they experience enormous financial and competitive pressures that threaten their ability to earn and save enough money to survive, adapt and live a good life with their family, especially when they include 25+ years of old age with their spouse.

Eventually, the pressures win and businesspeople and businesses become open to adopting new knowledge, new DMRVPs, or new language, that enables them to compete successfully enough to fulfill their financial, career and business intentions.

Aji is new knowledge. It is new:

Language

DMRVPs that enable computers and the internet to be used strategically

Ideas and practices

Intentions to produce outcomes along with the new skills needed to fulfill those intentions

To increase their competitive knowledge, businesspeople learn Aji's explanations and stories, or Aji's new DMRVP, action package and ideas about human beings and how to make money using computers and the internet in the most rapidly changing, intensely competitive, increasingly complex and technologically advanced global marketplace in history.

Where does learning, or accumulating capabilities to produce intended outcomes such as doubling one's income, begin?

A human being's knowledge to produce outcomes in given situations begins with their *orientation* in life, or way of being.

People's orientations determine if and how they relate to their concerns, situations, capabilities and strategies for the sake of surviving, adapting and living a good life with their family and in society.

Are businesspeople *being* serious, ambitious, trustworthy, dignified, caring, sincere, strategic and competitive, or are they *being* apathetic, prideful, task-oriented, process driven, satisfied with incremental improvements, arrogant, aimless, reactive and insincere about taking practical care of their family's concerns?

People's orientation is causal. It is people's fundamental way of being that shapes their thoughts and actions to produce outcomes and situations, such as doubling their incomes, or fail to produce them.

It's no coincidence that task-*oriented* businesspeople's intentions and skills are always organized around getting jobs done. It's 100% predictable.

The same is true about businesspeople who are *oriented* to rely on their common sense. The skills they learn to make money are always equally common, obvious, ordinary, uncompetitive and define mediocrity in IR#4.

Here's the way it works:

> Businesspeople's (1) *orientations* always produce their (2) *intentions to produce outcomes* and their (3) *willingness to invent or learn new business skills* to fulfill those intentions.

> When businesspeople are prideful and drifting aimlessly through their career, for instance, because they are indifferent about earning and saving enough money for 25+ years of old age with their spouse, they are unwilling to spend time, energy, money and lost opportunities to learn new skills.

> When their orientation changes, which usually happens when businesspeople complete Part #1 of The Strategy and constitute their life, financial and business ambitions with their spouse, learning Aji becomes *meaningful, easy, enjoyable and definitive.*

*****

Fantasy, Possibility and Opportunity

What Is a Fantasy, Possibility and Opportunity?

Popular Culture and Bullshitting

When People Bullshit, They…

What Is a Fantasy, Possibility and Opportunity?

(To Avoid a Chronic Lack of Power)

A *fantasy* is… a notion about producing a future situation that cannot be produced, such as earning a living or becoming rich while running a hot dog stand or using one's common sense to compete in IR#4.

A notion is a fantasy when a person can come up with *one practical reason* why a situation cannot be produced.

A *possibility* is… a notion about producing a future situation that is judged to be within a person's capacity to produce because there is *no reason* why it cannot.

Once a possibility exists, people can speculate on how much of a possibility really exists.

An *opportunity* is… a *real structure* for the fulfillment or production of a situation.

Once an opportunity exists, real action to produce an outcome exists, too. Then, people can speculate about its importance, utility and worth to help them produce outcomes that fulfill their intentions.

Here's a practical example:

Fantasy   When a state does not offer a lottery, winning the lottery is a *fantasy*. It's just an idea.

Possibility   When a state offers a lottery, a real structure exists that makes winning the lottery a *possibility* for people who live in that state.

Opportunity   When someone buys a lottery ticket, they produce a specific situation that is a *real opportunity* for them to win the lottery.

The same types of claims exist for *earning a living, or becoming rich,* when working in a global marketplace organized around the ubiquitous use of computers and the internet.

Fantasy   When Aji does not exist and businesspeople rely on their common sense, hard work, busyness and bullshit about their finances, career and business,

   … earning and saving "enough money" to live a good life in IR#4 is a *fantasy*.

Possibility   When Aji exists in the marketplace,

   … learning how to use it to double one's income enough to earn a living with a Normal IR#4 Income becomes a *possibility*.

Opportunity   When businesspeople learn how to use a competitive, fundamental strategy such as Aji, and learn how to use four fundamental tactics to execute The Strategy -- designing new offers, practices, narratives and strategies,

   … earning a living, and becoming rich, becomes an *opportunity*.

The marketplace *drifts* from state to state in terms of *fantasies, possibilities* and *opportunities* because the evolution of human capabilities changes what is, and is not, possible over time.

Fantasies → Possibilities → Opportunities

This means that our opportunities to *make valuable offers* to fulfill financial ambitions to produce wealth and live a good life *change* as the marketplace's competitive capabilities, advantages and situations evolve.

When using IR#3 business orientations, intentions and skills no longer produces competitive advantages, continuing to use them makes it impossible to produce:

Marginal utilities that are fresh, new, highly valued and scarce relative to demand

Competitive advantages, monopolies and auctions

Autonomy

Identities of trust and value

Highly compensated leadership roles

Organizations for accumulating power

And with the end of the above comes the end of:

High incomes

Capital-at-work for retirement

Doubling enterprise values

Without opportunities to increase their competitive capabilities and advantages, because they cannot distinguish popular business fantasies from real possibilities and opportunities to make money with their computers and the internet,

… businesspeople suffer from a chronic lack of power in the marketplace and at home,

… and cannot increase their productivity, value and incomes.

Using Aji creates a new opportunity for businesspeople and business organizations to fulfill their financial, career and business intentions, including saving enough to afford the goods and services they are certain to need during 25+ years of old age with their spouse.

Fantasy, Possibility and Opportunity

Popular Culture and Bullshitting

Pop culture and *bullshitting* are serious problems for businesspeople until they become easy and obvious to observe. The reasons they exist and are produced, as well as the serious breakdowns businesspeople create for themselves and their family when they accept their orientations, intentions and skills, are not obvious.

To succeed in IR#4 and double productivity, value and incomes, businesspeople need to see them clearly and eschew both of them,

… except when going about normal and ordinary business such as grocery shopping and entertainment.

Both confuse fantasies, possibilities and real opportunities and are misleading about how and why to make "enough money" to qualify as "earning a living", when 25+ years of old age with one's spouse is included.

They pander to people by encouraging them to misbehave and feel victimized and entitled instead of accepting personal responsibility for their life and behaving with dignity.

Both sell "happy stories" that are false narratives, or seductive fantasies, about what happens in the future when people don't take care of their finances and dignity that tranquilize people, as if there are no consequences they really need to care about.

Scientists, doctors and psychologists tell a different story. They know the facts and truths.

They say that the moment people realize they don't have enough money saved for old age, chronic financial stress begins.

Desperation increases.

Hardships grow relentlessly and people's health suffers.

Existential despair grips people.

Marriages dissolve.

Children become resentful.

People become ill and their lifespans are shortened by as much as 20 years.

On the other hand, no one forces businesspeople to accept pop culture and join in.

Only basic arithmetic that most people learn in junior high school is needed to add up how much food, housing, medical care and transportation cost for a year.

Multiply how much they cost by 25 years (without inflation) to determine how much annual income is needed after taxes to afford them and it's obvious that businesspeople who lack a pension must save millions of dollars before they can retire without fear of running out of food with their spouse before they die.

Popular culture is not about being adult, dignified, serious about one's life or competitive. Nor is it about how to earn a living in IR#4, or become rich, when using computers and the internet.

It's about, and for, ordinary people who are going about their lives doing the ordinary things all human beings do to survive, adapt and live a good life such as buy, cook and eat food; fix up their homes; borrow money to buy a car; buy health insurance; or find family entertainment.

Fundamentally, culture is about economics.

Plop a group of people down in some location and together they'll figure out the best ways to eat, build homes, constitute marriages, raise and educate children, and celebrate accomplishments.

To keep costs down, they'll use local produce, share their favorite recipes, dress with the same material and clothes, invent their own jargon.

Everyone is ordinary sometimes, even geniuses, celebrities and the super-rich.

We are all ordinary, for instance, when we go to an ordinary grocery store to buy ordinary groceries, put on our pants, love our children, feel cold or ill, or when we watch ordinary television shows in ordinary ways.

So, learning about prices or the best television shows from popular culture can be useful to keep our costs down and our returns high.

But how to earn a living without a pension, which means having to earn and save enough money to avoid running out of it with one's spouse until he or she is 90 years old, while using a computer and the internet as one's primary moneymaking tools in the most rapidly changing and intensely competitive global marketplace in history,

  ... is not ordinary.

That's why businesspeople who rely on popular culture's happy stories, books, shows, courses, seminars and theories about how to make money that are old, common, obvious, false and obsolete fail to fulfill their financial intentions.

That's why businesspeople who are serious about taking care of their most fundamental and practical human concerns avoid popular culture's business offers and free advice,

... and seek out something like Aji instead.

Pop culture often manipulates businesspeople by trying to convince them that they aren't nearly as happy as they should be, need to be or want to be when they are working to earn a living or saving their money for old age.

It repeats, for instance, that what businesspeople really need to do to be happy is buy different forms of entertainment to distract them from reality because YOLO (you only live once).

It promotes fantasies intended to mislead about what does, and does not, make people happy. It even misrepresents the true nature of human happiness.

It confuses and overrates the real possibilities and actual benefits of earning a top 1% glamorous income.

How people's guts feel in competitive situations, for example, is not a "Source of Power", and *human happiness is about being content with one's life at home and with society*, rather than jumping up and down with adrenaline-filled excitement as we see on game shows, sports contests and politics.

The real reason ordinary businesspeople become rich, by the way, has nothing to with wanting to live a glamorous television life and everything to do with taking better than satisfactory care of their spouse and children.

Pop culture panders to people by encouraging them to misbehave and indulge their psychology. It supports and advises people to bullshit at home and at work because it's easy, lowers costs in the moment, is often tolerated and seems to be effective some of the time, unless you look at the incomes, families, identities, accomplishments and leadership roles bullshitters really produce.

You know, if it feels right… trust your gut… you deserve it!… YOLO… you're entitled!

The truth about bullshitting is simple:

Bullshitting ruins businesspeople's competitive capabilities and advantages.

It makes establishing identities of *superior trustworthiness, value, authority, leadership and dignity* impossible.

The essence of bullshit, according to Harry Frankfurt, professor emeritus at Princeton University, where he taught for 12 years, and the author of *On Bullshit*, ***is speaking without regard for the truth or being concerned with how things really are to get away with something.***

Bullshitters can be very persuasive, entertaining, charming, clever, intelligent and even artistic in the way they weave their claims.

They can even be bullshit artists who have large followings online who admire how they do it.

Nevertheless, they are bullshitting people, which is an aggressive, insulting and harmful way of speaking. It is undignified and disregards and misrepresents the truth about people and reality. It promulgates falsehoods.

Bullshit drives businesspeople crazy and weakens their ability to take care of themselves and their families.

Bullshit is a way of speaking to* other *people.

No one can bullshit themselves. No one can fool themselves about the truth any more than they can make themselves forget a joke so they can laugh at it again. It is not possible.

When people bullshit, they know *exactly* what they are doing but they often don't realize it's called "bullshit".

When bullshitters pretend they didn't realize they were bullshitting, or claim they were bullshitting themselves, too, ***they are bullshitting some more.***

When People Bullshit...

They...

Misrepresent their true intentions, or what they are really up to accomplishing, and try to manipulate their listeners, even if what they do say is true, ***to get away with something*** such as cutting their costs and shifting burdens, obligations and commitments to others.

Pretend to be friendly, sincere, honest, thoughtful, caring and helpful when nothing could be further from the truth. Pretending to be sincere is part of bullshitting, including the apologies bullshitters make when they are caught in the act.

Harm their listeners by creating a false or dishonest narrative about what their real intentions are, and what they know or believe to be real and true.

May not know misrepresenting their intentions to get away with something is called "bullshitting".

Don't care at all about the consequences they produce for those who believe them, even if it ruins their family, finances and life.

One way to combat popular culture and bullshitting is to become clear about what they are,

> ... the consequences they produce to fulfilling businesspeople's financial, career and business intentions to live a good life,

> ... and the *practical* differences between *fantasies, possibilities* and *opportunities*.

*****

What Is Money?

What Is Money?

Currency DOES NOT = Money

5 Ways to Transact

Gift giving

Exchanging Favors

Barter

Trade

Currency

What Is Money?

The first claim to accept and remember about money is that *it is not currency.*

The second is that *"money" is any form of HELP* -- OPNS, including goods and services -- *that people want badly enough to pay for.*

> This includes goods and services such as food in grocery stores, electricity for people's homes, gasoline, medicine, school teachers, new tires, clothing, water, etc.

> It also includes HELP fulfilling financial, career and business intentions that employees, colleagues, customers, vendors and employers offer one another to earn a living.

> *Any form of HELP that people are willing to pay for is real money.*

Computers and the internet are the best moneymaking tools ever invented, by far.

> *No other tool ever invented comes close.*

> And… *every businessperson can afford to own one.*

> The problem is that how to use them to make money is not obvious, perceivable or common sense.

Computers don't announce their value, though, or why and how they can be used to make money. It's important to remember that they have no intention to help anyone. They are devices or artifacts.

They don't move, so we can't see what they do or anticipate the outcomes they can be used to produce.

In fact, they don't *do* anything, ever. They just sit until they are used. They are tools. They are "things".

They are just as happy being used to complete tasks, earn too little money or as a door stop.

How to "make money" with a computer is not obvious, perceivable or common sense.

The new orientations, intentions to produce outcomes and business skills used to fulfill those intentions with computers are new and not common sense.

They must be learned.

Aji explains and shows businesspeople how it's done.

One of the first things businesspeople need to know before they can execute The Strategy to *double* their productivity, value and incomes,

> … is that their "money" *is* their offers, practices, narratives and strategies,

> … including the goods and services whose help to take care of their concerns, situations, capabilities and strategies others want badly enough to pay for.

In the same way a hammer can be used to hammer nails or as a paperweight or doorstop, depending upon the user's intentions to produce an outcome, computers can be used to get jobs done, which suppresses businesspeople's incomes by 100%, or to execute a competitive, fundamental strategy, which doubles productivity, value and incomes.

> *It all depends upon businesspeople's intentions to produce an outcome, or to make enough money, when they use their computers and the internet.*

If businesspeople are satisfied with using their computer to earn a Normal IR#3 Income, even though it is only half as much as they could earn if they used Aji to make money and they can't save enough money to avoid running out of it with their spouse during 25+ years of old age,

... *their computer doesn't care.*

But, if they are concerned about earning and saving "enough money" to survive day-to-day, adapt over time as their bodies and circumstances change, and live a good life with their spouse until they are at least 90 years old,

... their computer and the internet can be used to fulfill that purpose, too.

Currency DOES NOT = Money

This is a form of cognitive dissonance.

It thwarts fulfilling financial intentions.

When businesspeople confuse money with currency, they suffer from a form of cognitive dissonance that suppresses their productivity, value and incomes by at least 100%.

> That is, when they go to work with the intention to "make money" and think money is currency, the only way they can "make it" is to use a printing press, which is absurd.

> This is a real problem for businesspeople and businesses now that computers, computer-driven devices and the internet are their primary moneymaking tools.

Global competitors don't confuse making money with making currency. They know money is the scarce offers, practices, narratives and strategies (OPNS) people need to help them to take care of their *concerns*, cope with *situations*, increase their *capabilities* to produce outcomes and perform *strategies* to fulfill their intentions.

> They are not confused about the nature and operations of money, which is why they get rich, of course. What's important is that in the process of making money with new OPNS, they also establish new standards of value with their goods and services for everyone else that cannot be matched when businesspeople continue to rely on their common sense, hard work and IR#3 business skills.

* * * * *

5 Ways to Transact

Money is **HELP** people need, or want, to take care of their concerns, situations, capabilities and strategies, that is highly valued and scarce relative to demand.

This is a complex and abstract idea or concept.

It is not simple, obvious, perceivable, objective, concrete or easy to understand.

No one can figure this out with their common sense.

When businesspeople listen to popular culture's bullshit explanations about money, they often end up thinking that money is simple, obvious and concrete, and confuse it with currency.

This makes it impossible for them to understand how to make money to take care of their family.

Currency is *not* "real" money. It is a tool societies use *as if* it is money to lower the cost of transactions, which makes it easier to make money.

When people "have money",

> ... it means they have a form of HELP such as a good or service,

> ... or an offer, practice, narrative or strategy (OPNS),

> ... that is a way to produce an outcome that someone else wants and values enough to give them something in return, or to pay a purchase price.

Currency is a concrete financial *tool*. It is a thing we can carry around. Using currency is much easier than bartering and trading, but it is *not* money. It is an artifact that societies create and use *as if* it was money.

> This lowers the cost to buy and sell goods and services, or to transact and "make money".

Put another way, when businesspeople confuse currency with money they also confuse themselves, because the only possible way to "make money" is to use a printing press.

> It just makes matters worse to try and figure out how a head of lettuce, for example, could actually be worth a dollar bill, or why a car is worth thousands of them. The bill, or the currency, is totally useless unless people agree to *pretend* it has value. It won't taste good in a salad or on a hamburger.

The truth is that real money, which is always different forms of HELP, actually has real, practical value in the world even though the notion is abstract.

Real money may be invisible, or an idea, but when the HELP you can provide is fresh, new, highly valued and scarce relative to demand,

… it has the power to compel people, businesses and even countries to give you something you want in return.

From economists' point of view, there is no difference between a human being going to the grocery store with the purpose of buying a head of lettuce and the grocery store that puts out lettuce with the intention of buying people's currency.

The fundamentals are identical.

People "make money" when they transact.

There's no other way to do it.

If whatever purchase price they get in return for their good or service, or OPNS, increases their capabilities to take care of their family or fulfill their intentions, they "made money".

This is also called "making a profit".

The 5 Forms of Making Money

#1 - *Exchanging currency* for a good or service is only one form of money.

The other forms of money/HELP are:

#2 - *Barter* (2 parties)   I'll trade you my old computer in return for your old printer.

#3 - *Trade* (3 or more parties)   (Barter conversations in a sequence)

#4 - *Gift giving*   Here's some help on how to execute The Strategy. You can help me some other time…

#5 - *Exchanging favors*   I'll help you design your offers if you'll help me design mine.

Businesspeople and businesses use all five forms of making money to fulfill their financial, career and business intentions. Using them is easy, enjoyable and definitive. They "work".

They use them to transact and build their identities with customers, employers, employees, colleagues and vendors.

*****

Introductory Aji Distinctions, Focuses and Facts

Building the Frame

We Are Living in The Fourth Industrial Revolution (IR#4)

Building the Frame Continued…

Fundamental Claims About Financial Realities

Income, Capital and Knowledge Gaps

Introductory Aji Distinctions and Facts

Building the Frame

To understand how or why human beings think and act as they do to make money, and why it is, and is not, possible to make more, isn't possible without first understanding the situation, or "frame" of circumstances, in which people find themselves *from their point of view.*

This is because people's situations -- the threats they must avoid, the obligations they must fulfill and the opportunities they must exploit --

… shape and limit their possibilities to think and act to produce outcomes to fulfill their intentions.

A *"frame"* is *a narrative about the circumstances that will shape people's thoughts and actions to produce an outcome that fulfills an intention.*

Its purpose is to help a Listener think and act effectively in the circumstances to fulfill their intentions,

… or to coordinate their thoughts and actions with other followers to fulfill their shared intentions.

A frame is built by first stating the *outcome to be produced* or the *intention to be fulfilled*,

> … such as lowering costs, increasing market share or doubling one's income.

Then people speak the:

> *Concerns* that must be cared for such as quality or trustworthiness
>
> *Situations* in which action will occur, i.e., threats to avoid, obligations to fulfill and opportunities to exploit
>
> *Capabilities* needed to produce intended outcomes
>
> *Strategies*, or action plans, that are already known or will be invented, to produce outcomes
>
> > … so that Listeners can design offers, practices, narratives and strategies they'll need to cope with them.

A frame is also an ***"exposition"***, or the first part of a business narrative, which is explained more fully elsewhere in these notes.

> In short, the exposition is the beginning of a narrative that constitutes the purpose or topic of the narrative and frames the circumstances in which people will act.
>
> The other parts of a narrative are its Conflict, Rising Action, Resolution and Denouement.

When businesspeople use a business narrative's *exposition* to create a frame, they tell their Listeners or Followers:

1. *The Speaker's* (their) identities, TVAL&D

2. *The Champion's* identities

3. *The Major Actors* who will help

4. *The Minor Actors* who will help

5. *The Adversaries*, or sources of breakdowns and thwarted intentions, with which they must cope

6. *The Current Situation's* threats to avoid, obligations to fulfill and opportunities to exploit

7. *The Situation that Starts Action*, now, to produce a highly valued return

8. *The Conflict* or unsatisfactory situation to be fixed

9. *The Resolution* that ends action and investment, and starts returns

10. *The Denouement*, or new space of possibilities for thought and action that is always the real purpose of action and transaction

For instance, people out camping who see a 500 lb. black bear sneaking up behind them think and act differently than the people sitting right next to them who don't see the bear. Then remember the child who sees the bear and thinks it's cute and cuddly.

They are in different situations even though they are sitting next to each other. They are living in different stories about their circumstances and ability to survive and adapt in the next few minutes.

Because of their different interpretations about their situation, they see different *threats* to avoid, *obligations* to fulfill and *opportunities* to exploit.

We know all of it is interpretation, and that none of it is obvious or objectively true, because the child who sees the bear just as clearly as any adult wants to give it a hug.

The same claim is true about IR#3 businesspeople and IR#4 businesspeople who use Aji.

They are in the exact same global marketplace, use the same tools, but have completely different interpretations about the threats they need to avoid, the obligations to fulfill and the opportunities they can exploit to double their incomes.

Aji is a new frame that enables businesspeople to double their productivity, value and incomes in IR#4 using their computers and the internet.

It shows businesspeople "the bears" (global competitors, new tools, strategic orientations, task orientation, reliance on common sense and too low productivity, value, income and savings) sneaking up behind them. Then it shows them the actions to take to deal with them, which is to use a competitive, fundamental strategy.

Using Aji enables businesspeople, and entire businesses, to think, act and work in a new frame of possibilities that computers and the internet make possible.

When businesspeople use Aji, the marketplace explodes with new opportunities they can exploit to double their incomes.

IR#3 businesspeople who sit next to them have no idea the opportunities exist.

That's why The Strategy has businesspeople become clear about the truths and facts that predetermine what their financial intentions *must be* -- minimally, to afford food, housing, medical care and transportation until they die -- and what is, and is not, possible to accomplish their objective.

This is businesspeople's new frame, or space of possibilities for thought and action in IR#4. They *must* honor it to take care of their survival and ability to adapt with their spouse until they are at least 90 years old.

When businesspeople speak their intentions to produce an outcome while understanding what is, and is not, possible, as well as what is required, forbidden and allowed in order to produce an outcome,

... they produce a frame for their thinking, speaking and acting to fulfill their intentions that produces "good aji", or is likely to work.

* "Good aji" is having the potential to win. You can read about it in ***What Does Aji Mean?*** at the start of this volume.

The same thing is true about industrial revolutions.

To earn a living or become rich in them, businesspeople must understand the new frame of *competitive* concerns, situations, capabilities and strategies (CSCS) in which they find themselves:

What is, and is not, possible right now using computers and the internet to make money, and why?

What are the threats to avoid, obligations to fulfill and opportunities to exploit to double productivity, value and incomes?

What thoughts, actions and outcomes are required, forbidden and allowed to make money when using computers and the internet?

Like 500 lb. bears, industrial revolutions are very dangerous, do not announce their presence or intentions, and are indifferent to the consequences they cause to businesspeople and their families.

They are dangerous because they change everyone's space of possibilities to make enough money to:

1. *Survive* day to day

2. *Adapt* over time as our bodies and circumstances change

3. *Live a good life* with our spouse and children until we are at least 90 years old without running out of money

The businesspeople and businesses who don't see the danger of IR#4's competitive situations, who don't understand it or who don't care about it in the moment, can't earn and save "enough money" to avoid running out of it with their spouse long before they die.

One day they wake up and realize what has happened... *and it's too late to fix.*

They don't have enough money saved to afford the food, housing, medical care and transportation they are certain to need with their spouse in order to survive, adapt and live a good life during 25+ years of old age and... *it's too late to fix.*

They can't keep their marriage vows to take care of their spouse's most fundamental and practical human concerns such as their health 'til death do us part... *and it's too late to fix.*

They become a "parent tax", or financial burden, on their children, their in-laws and their grandchildren when they don't have enough money for food, housing, medical care and transportation... *you know the rest.*

We Are Living in The Fourth Industrial Revolution (IR#4)

It is a new frame of financial and competitive *threats* businesspeople need to avoid, *obligations* they need to fulfill and *opportunities* they need to exploit if they are to earn a living, or become rich.

Local and global competitors have created the most rapidly changing, competitive, complex and technologically advanced global marketplace in history. They know how to use their computers strategically and competitively as Aji shows, rather than with task orientation and common sense.

They churn out steady streams of fresh, new offers, practices, narratives and strategies (OPNS) throughout the day, every day, on the internet for everyone to see that change everyone's frame by setting new standards for value in the marketplace for everyone.

This means that the criteria and standards people and businesses use to assess value,

> … or what they consider to be important, useful and worthwhile to buy and use,

> … that they need to buy quickly and pay a premium for because the supply is limited,

> … changes throughout the day in as little as 15 minutes as they learn about new OPNS via the internet.

The distinctions that follow introduce Aji's intentions to *double* productivity, value and incomes and build the frame in which businesspeople think, speak their commitments and act to fulfill their specific financial intentions.

Together, they begin to explain the descriptions, meanings, relevance, value and purposes of computers and the internet in IR#4's competitive situations.

They begin to explain the frame of threats to avoid, obligations to fulfill and opportunities to exploit in IR#4 that make it possible for businesspeople to *double* productivity, value and incomes.

In other words, they begin to explain the "bears" sneaking up on businesspeople in IR#4 so they can be avoided and their incomes *doubled*.

To a person or business, IR#4 competitors are ambitious, thoughtful, strategic and competitive when they use their computers and the internet.

They are not IR#3 competitors who are task-oriented as they drift without aim through their jobs and careers, who rely on their commonsense, are too busy to learn, who focus on processes and procedures, and are impressed with incremental improvements.

They are working inside a different interpretation about what is *forbidden, required* and *allowed* to make money with computers and the internet that is twice as competitive as IR#3's business skills.

Use the following Aji distinctions and claims to re-design your frame, or the:

1. ***Competitive threats you intend to avoid*** because they will:

    Thwart your intentions

    Cause physical harm

2. ***Competitive obligations you intend to fulfill*** to:

    Keep existing opportunities to make money

    Produce new opportunities to make money

    Avoid avoidable costs and risks to make money

3. ***Competitive opportunities you intend to exploit*** to make money, such as Aji, to:

    Take care of *concerns*

    Cope with *situations*

    Increase *capabilities*

    Design and execute *strategies*

    … to fulfill your financial, career and business intentions.

Introductory Aji Distinctions and Facts

Building the Frame Continued...

Every thought and action businesspeople perform to execute *The Aji Source Fundamental Strategy* is aimed at fulfilling these three fundamental objectives:

Ultimate Ambitions

To earn, save and invest enough money to survive, adapt to change and live a good life to:

Afford the goods and services businesspeople will need for food, housing, medical care and transportation with their spouse

Fulfill their marriage vows

Fulfill their parenting commitments

Live with dignity in society

... until they are at least 90 years old

Strategic Objectives	To increase their competitive capabilities and advantages, productivity, value and incomes, and enterprise values
Tactical Focuses	To produce a steady stream of *offers, practices, narratives* and *strategies* that are (1) fresh, (2) new, (3) highly valued and (4) scarce relative to demand -- their marginal utilities are *un*common, strategic and *superior* to *common* ones

Fundamental Claims About Financial Realities

1. *Permanent human concerns* such as housing, food, transportation, medical care, family and play, *cost money. Always.* They must be taken care of to a satisfactory standard, or people cannot survive and adapt as their bodies and situations change.

   They do not change as we age.

   They cannot be ignored or avoided without triggering desperation, despair, chronic stress, suffering, bad health and shortened lifespans.

2. *People must earn and save "enough money" to afford what economists call non-discretionary goods and services* -- food, housing, medical care and transportation -- to (1) survive in the moment and (2) adapt over time as their bodies and environment change until they are at least 90 years old.

   Only having "enough money" when they retire enables businesspeople and their spouses to avoid chronic financial stress that ruins their health and shortens their lifespans by as much as 20 years.

   It enables people to (1) keep their marriage vows, (2) keep their parenting commitments and (3) live with dignity in society.

3. *Prices for goods and services everyone requires* to survive, adapt over time and live a good life *are determined by supply and demand* regardless of our age, need, illness, importance or how much money we used to earn.

   When businesspeople run out of money, or know that will happen in the future, what they really run out of is food, housing, medical care, transportation, peace of mind and freedom to do anything other than focus on their survival and ability to adapt.

4. *Longevity,* or how long people are expected to live, *is currently about 85 years*, or 25+ years after the infirmities of old age begin to assert themselves at age 60.

5. *Average stock market returns* of 8% *double investments every 10 years.*

6. *Average inflation of 3%* reduces real returns to 5% (8% - 3%), so *the real purchasing power of money halves every 15 years.*

7. *Maximum withdrawal amount from invested savings is 4%.*

   Every $1m saved and invested passively = $40k annual income.

   A $100k annual income requires $2.5m passively invested.

Income, Capital and Knowledge Gaps in IR#4

Annual Income Gap   The difference between how much people earn and the amount they need to earn to save and invest enough to survive, adapt over time and live a good life with their spouse their *entire* life

Capital-at-Work Gap   The difference between how much people have invested and the amount they need to have invested to be *minimally* or *fully* on track to have enough money saved by age 60

Knowledge Gap   The difference between the knowledge people have that produces *insufficient* annual income and capital-at-work,

        … and the amount required to increase their incomes enough to bridge their gaps,

        … to fulfill their life, financial and business ambitions to survive, adapt over time and live a good life

        *****

* * * * *

"How Much Money Is Enough?" Calculation

Building the Frame

About the Financial and Psychological Shock...

"How Much Money Is Enough?" Calculation

"How Much Money Is Enough?" Calculation

Building the Frame

Some goods and services are non-discretionary, according to economists, doctors and scientists, which means *people have no choice but to buy them* or they and their spouse will die.

If you reflect, you'll see that the entire global marketplace is organized around taking care of these fundamental human concerns.

The **four categories of non-discretionary goods and services** everyone must be able to afford to a satisfactory standard every day of their life are:

Food	Grocery stores
Housing	Mortgage/rent, insurance, utilities, property taxes, daily maintenance, long-term maintenance
Medical Care	Out of pocket, deductibles, insurance, Medicare
Transportation	Loans, insurance, gasoline, taxes, servicing, long-term maintenance

Earning and saving enough money to afford non-discretionary goods and services is part of the frame in IR#4 because businesspeople who do not have pensions now expect to live 25+ years with their spouse after they retire.

> Businesspeople must save enough money during their career to afford those goods and services to survive, adapt and live a good life, including old age.
>
> In other words, *anything* businesspeople are thinking, speaking about, committing to or acting to produce that is inconsistent with making "enough money" to afford those goods and services with their spouse until they are at least 90 years old,
>
> > ... *makes no sense*,
>
> > ... *and is counterproductive* because it will cause suffering, despair and bad health, rather than support businesspeople's intentions to live a good life.

The four categories of goods and services, or human concerns, are non-discretionary because human beings need them available 24/7 to:

1. *Survive* day to day

2. *Adapt over time* as their bodies and circumstances change

3. *Live a good life* with their spouse and children until they are at least 90 years old

Most businesspeople say they need annual incomes well above $100k to afford a satisfactory amount of good quality non-discretionary goods and services.

Since the maximum amount people can withdraw from their savings without running out of it before they die, if it is invested passively, is 4%, they must have $2.5m saved to produce $100k annually today.

Because of 3% average inflation, that amount becomes $3.75m for 46-year-olds and $5m for 36-year-olds.

When businesspeople run out of money with their spouse during old age, it triggers *chronic financial stress,* which is unhealthy, makes living a good life impossible and shortens people's lifespans by as much as 20 years.

The stress comes from being unable to afford sufficient food, housing, medical care and transportation to take care of people's biological concerns for their body.

The stress is "chronic" because it is unrelenting and cannot be fixed. People live in it 24/7 and can't escape it.

It is characterized by psychologists, economists and philosophers as increasing and unstoppable hardships, desperation, despair, suffering and pain as people age. It makes people ill and shortens their lifespans.

When businesspeople love their spouse, running out of money and being unable to take care of their spouse's most important, practical and fundamental human concerns can trigger *existential despair* as they age, or the sense that their life had no meaning.

When businesspeople love their children, running out of money makes them a "parent tax", or financial burden, that ruins their children's chances of earning and saving enough money to live a good life with their spouse and children.

This situation can also trigger existential despair.

Consequently, it is important for businesspeople *and their spouses* to know how much money they *really* need to earn and save to afford the goods and services they are certain to need until they are at least 90 years old.

It helps when businesspeople and their spouses remember their vows.

Does fulfilling their vows include being ignorant, passive, apathetic or disinterested in earning and saving enough money to avoid running out of it so their spouse has to go without food, housing, medical care or transportation, before they are at least 90 years old?

It helps if both spouses are clear about their parenting commitments, too.

Do they intend to raise their children so they can earn a living with their computers and the internet?

If so, they need to learn how to do it themselves first.

Do they intend to avoid becoming a "parent tax", or financial burden, on their children, in-laws and grandchildren?

If so, how much money do they need to earn and save to accomplish this?

About the financial and psychological shock…

The huge amounts of money businesspeople *really* need to earn and save in IR#4 to live a good life with their spouse and children is often a shock.

In IR#3, businesspeople's biggest assets were their car and house.

In IR#4, businesspeople's savings for old age dwarf the value of their car and home.

It takes most businesspeople and their spouses a few weeks to adjust to how much they really need to increase their productivity, value and incomes to save enough money to afford 25+ years of old age together.

Then, they use Aji to deal with the situation to produce a life that is deeply meaningful, satisfying, worthwhile and enjoyable from their point of view,

… instead of one dominated by increasing hardships, chronic financial stresses and suffering.

"How Much Money Is Enough?" Calculation

#1 – Write down your annual income minus annual savings

Income $220k, Savings $20k
*Income after savings $200k = **Current standard of living***

Distinctions:
Earn
Survive
Adapt to biological and external changes
Live a good life without compromise

#2 – Multiply #1 by 25 (4% Rule)

*$200k x 25 = $5m = **Capital-at-Work (CAW)*** required to
                              maintain standard of living for 25+
                              years of old age

Distinctions:
Capital-at-work
Net worth
Fiduciary responsibility
Monte Carlo calculations

#3 – If your age is closer to…

48, multiply #2 by 1.5 – *Inflation adjusted*

38, multiply by 2

28, multiply by 2.75

Distinctions:
Inflation

#4 – Subtract #3 from your current capital-at-work

Current capital-at-work = $500k

10m - $500k = $9.5m = **CAW gap**

#5 – Subtract your age from 60 – *calculate space for producing income*

60 - 44 = 16 years = **Time available to bridge any financial gap**

#6 – *Divide #4 by #5* – *calculate annual CAW gap*

*$9.5m ÷ 16 years = $679k = **Annual CAW gap***

#7 – *Multiply #6 by 2* – *include taxes*

*2 x $679k = $1.4m = **Annual income required to bridge gap***

Background facts:

250 working days per year

365 days – 104 weekend days and 11 holidays

2,000 working hours per year

250 days x 8 hours

*****

* * * * *

4 Fundamental Actions

IR#4 Businesspeople Use Every Day

to Make Money

Learning, Communicating, Coordinating and Producing

#1 - Competitive *Learning* to produce new outcomes

#2 - *Communicating* Commitments and Interpretations

#3 - *Coordinating* Thought and Action

#4 - Producing New Offers, Practices, Narratives and Strategies

Learning, Communicating, Coordinating and Producing

Everyday business is specifically different for individual businesspeople as they cope with whatever specific competitive situation exists for them at the time. IR#4's rapidly changing competitive situations are complex and becoming more complex every day because businesspeople are using computers and the internet to make money in a global marketplace, even if they don't realize it.

Increasing complexity is predictable in competitive situations because it often increases the capabilities of a tool, or of an offer, practice, narrative or strategy (OPNS), or a good or service.

Computers and the internet are becoming more complex every day. They make increasing the complexity of new OPNS easy to do and low cost.

Consequently, businesspeople need to anticipate that OPNS in the marketplace, including goods and services, will become more complex and competitive over time.

To compete, businesspeople and business organizations must constantly increase their competitive capabilities and advantages to design, make and use fresh, new OPNS strategically and competitively.

Fundamentally, however, there exist only four actions businesspeople actually use and perform throughout the day to make money, no matter what specific competitive situations exist in the moment:

1. ***Learning*** to produce new outcomes in new competitive situations

2. ***Communicating*** explanations, commitments, interpretations, intentions, etc.

3. ***Coordinating*** thought and action to increase productivity and value

4. ***Producing*** outcomes with steady streams of new offers, practices, narratives and strategies (OPNS)

    … that they use strategically and competitively.

Knowing this is an incredibly important competitive capability in rapid change.

It means businesspeople and entire businesses must build these four skills to become and continue to be competitive enough to fulfill their financial, career and business intentions.

The more skillful businesspeople become at using them, the more able they become at executing The Strategy and *doubling* their productivity, value and incomes as the competitive situations in which they find themselves change and become more complex.

4 Fundamental Actions

IR#4 Businesspeople Use Every Day

To Make Money

#1 - Competitive learning to produce new outcomes

Competitive learning's purpose is twofold:

1. To continually accumulate new **competitive capabilities**, or **business skills**, needed to produce *new competitive outcomes* (OPNS) needed to compete effectively in the top 1% of the marketplace

2. To produce, maintain and increase **competitive advantages**, which are the superior value of their OPNS's marginal utilities, using a special set of *expert* learning practices

Competitive learning to produce new outcomes is a set of three practices IR#4 businesspeople learn and exploit throughout their careers to increase their competitive capabilities:

Recurrence

Reciprocation

Recursion

These three learning practices are used intentionally every day, all day, with Aji to accumulate the *strategic* knowledge and power businesspeople need to fulfill their personal ambitions and business missions.

3 Fundamental Competitive Learning Practices

1. Recurrence   Revisit distinctions and practices in different situations,

> … to produce different outcomes and fulfill different intentions,

> … e.g., using these notes in your Aji IFP to revisit how to design an offer or the importance of dignity.

2. Reciprocation   Notice and assess outcomes produced in the world by one's actions,

> … e.g., the new assessments are customers, employees and vendors making after using a new business strategy.

3. Recursion   Reflect and make interpretations, speculate, learn and design new actions to fulfill intentions,

> … e.g., speculating, and later concluding, that a new practice is too costly.

Common business knowledge is often focused on enabling businesspeople to function effectively and efficiently, rather than to *compete* by producing marginal utilities that are fresh, new, highly valued and scarce relative to demand as businesspeople need to do in IR#4.

IR#3's business laborers learn *common* learning skills in grade school and continue to use them throughout their careers.

This enables them to function in the marketplace but prevents them from competing effectively for top 1% annual incomes

... because *common* learning produces *common* sense and *common* knowledge,

... which results in the production of equally *common* offers, practices, narratives and strategies,

... that always triggers indifference to their value, causes pricing and *guarantees* only bottom 99% annual incomes can be earned.

#2 - ***Communicating explanations, commitments, interpretations and intentions***

Communicating is producing:

Commitments to produce outcomes, or results, and fulfill intentions.

Creating new action packages,

… i.e., ambitions, moods, explanations, distinctions, interpretations, intentions, commitments, practices and outcomes.

Shared *explanations* of descriptions, meanings, relevance, value and purposes.

Compelling and seductive *interpretations* about the purpose and value of newly designed offers, practices, narratives and strategies.

Shared *"backgrounds of obviousness"* about ambitions, concerns, situations and capabilities necessary to enable transactions and coordinated thought and action.

#3 - *Coordinating thought and action*

Coordinating thought and action is producing, or triggering, thoughts, interpretations, commitments and action with customers, employers, employees, colleagues and vendors that:

1. Share *common* objectives

2. Enable people to think, interpret, commit and act *together* to produce outcomes

3. Are tactical, strategic, competitive and harmonious

It is essential to produce, maintain and increase:

Competitive capabilities and advantages

Action packages

Superior value

Top 1% annual incomes

    … with offers, practices, narratives and strategies.

It is required to fulfill ambitions and commitments, build and exploit networks, produce *highly* valued accomplishments, hold *highly* compensated leadership roles, build powerful business organizations and anticipate future threats, obligations and opportunities.

#4 - *Producing a steady stream of new offers, practices, narratives, strategies, goods and services*

> … that are fresh, new, highly valued and scarce relative to demand

> … to keep transaction costs low and purchase prices, or compensation, as high as possible

> … and that can be used to execute The Strategy.

Production of new goods and services -- offers, practices, narratives and strategies (OPNS) -- is how IR#4 businesspeople produce *superior* value for customers, employers, employees and colleagues.

Every Good and Service,

> … is an offer, practice, narrative and strategy that

> … is designed, sold, manufactured and distributed using OPNS.

The more *expert* or powerful IR#4 businesspeople's business narratives are,

> … the more able they become to produce a steady stream of *new* OPNS

> … that are scarce relative to demand, or *un*common, strategic and *superior* to *common* ones.

New OPNS produce *monopolies* that can be used to produce *auctions* that compel or seduce Buyers -- customers, employees, employers, colleagues and vendors -- to:

1. ***Accept offers easily and quickly,*** which produces *the lowest possible transaction costs*

2. ***Increase their willingness to pay a premium***, which produces *the highest possible purchase price*

*****

"HELP"

What Is "HELP"?

It is money.

"HELP"

… is fulfilling any of four intentions people interpret as help

Lower their costs: time, energy, money and lost opportunities

Make fulfilling their intentions possible

Improve the value of an outcome

Produce an outcome for people

What Is "HELP"?

It is money.

HELP people are willing to pay a purchase price for = Money

Human beings are animals. We are primates who speak. We make sense of our situations and design action to fulfill our intentions to survive, adapt and live a good life with language.

We are a social species whose individual members are unable to think and act autonomously to survive.

Consequently, people need HELP in every moment (even if they don't realize it) to take care of their most fundamental human concerns, e.g., food, housing, medical care and transportation, as well as family, work, educating children, socializing, play and dignity.

To get the help they need to survive, adapt and live a good life,

- … or to avoid increasing hardships, suffering, despair, illness and death,

- … human beings will transact, or give something in exchange.

Common help is priced low in the marketplace and produces Normal IR#3 Incomes that are too low to live a good life in IR#4.

HELP that is fresh, new, highly valued and scarce relative to demand produces Normal IR#4 Incomes that are twice as high. It compels Buyers to:

1. ***Accept quickly*** to produce the *lowest possible transaction costs*

2. ***Increase their willing to pay a premium*** to produce the *highest possible purchase price or compensation*

Both are used to double productivity, value and income.

Businesspeople can only transact and generate the highest possible purchase price (income) *if*, and only if,

... the offers, practices, narratives and strategies (OPNS) they design to HELP people are:

1. Fresh

2. New

3. Highly valued, important, useful and worth paying for

4. Scarce relative to demand

Businesspeople "make money" (literally), or double their productivity, value and incomes,

> … and earn Normal IR#4 Incomes,

> … when they design and execute OPNS that fulfill these four competitive conditions.

When their OPNS are common, traditional or ordinary, which means they define mediocrity,

> … the marketplace will price them much lower

> … and businesspeople find themselves earning a Normal IR#3 Income that is half as much as they could be earning.

Popular culture misleads businesspeople about the true practical importance of earning money. It shows heroes who don't need help to take care of their non-discretionary concerns for food, housing, medical care and transportation.

They never have to stop for food because they are never hungry or too tired, sick and unable to fly wherever they'd like.

Housing is just always there or isn't mentioned.

They shrug off injuries like bullet wounds as well as illnesses and the weaknesses they cause.

Transportation is always available just when they need it, or they can fly. They never have to wait a couple of hours for a bus.

They don't have to earn money to get what they need. It appears.

This isn't a problem when businesspeople remember they are watching simple high-concept fantasies and that in real life everyone needs a lot of money and help to survive day-to-day and adapt over time as their body ages in a marketplace that is competitive, complex and rapidly changing.

When businesspeople think they don't really need money and help, they drift through their jobs, decline to learn to increase their value, don't give or accept help that isn't shallow and cliched, and rely on their common sense.

This makes them weak, prideful, arrogant, jerky, untrustworthy and unable to lead in today's intensely competitive global marketplace.

How businesspeople think, what they believe to be true and their action packages are simple to hear when you know what to listen for.

There's a group of businesspeople who don't really think they need any help to make money, earn a living or become rich.

They work alone even when they work around hundreds of others because they don't allow anyone to affect how they think or what they do.

They don't learn. They don't succeed at saving enough money for their old age. They only pretend to have enough. Their family suffers the consequences of their arrogance, pride, too-low income and savings, and lack of dignity.

There's another group who participates in Aji IFPs so they can earn and save enough money to live a good life with their family, including saving enough money to afford 25+ years of old age with their spouse.

They work to help one another every day with their OPNS to build networks to increase their tactical, strategic and competitive capabilities and advantages.

They win. They succeed. They earn a living or become rich.

Their family prospers.

This is a fact of life for every human being.

In real life, *no one* can:

1. *Survive* from day to day

2. *Adapt* over time as their bodies and circumstances change

3. *Live a good life* with their family

> … without enough money to afford the HELP they need for food, housing, etc., every moment of every day.

From the food we eat, to the cars we drive, to the medicine we use, to the house we live in, to the clothes we wear, to the entertainment we enjoy… we need HELP.

To transact for the HELP to survive, adapt and live a good life that we all need from grocery stores, pharmacies, gas stations, utility companies, local governments, etc.,

> … we all need to have something of value to offer in return,

> … such as currency, trading something, doing a favor or giving a gift of help.

"HELP"

... is fulfilling any of four intentions people interpret as HELP

All customers, employers, employees, colleagues, vendors and competitors organize themselves around buying and selling the most helpful goods and services, or offers, practices, narratives and strategies (OPNS) they can find and produce.

Put another way, exchanging different forms of HELP such as paying the purchase price in a grocery store in return for dinner, or paying an employee in return for a service, is how human beings make money so they can survive, adapt as life changes and live a good life.

Here are the four fundamental intentions that people interpret as "HELP":

1. Increase the likelihood, or **make it possible**, for people to produce an outcome that fulfills their intentions

2. **Lower people's costs**, or reduce the time, energy, money or lost opportunities required to fulfill their intentions

3. Produce, or assist people, to **produce a better outcome** than they could have otherwise

4. **Produce an outcome for people**, or fulfill their intentions for them

The marketplace, as well as the underlying purpose and value of money, is based on transacting for the help people need to:

1. *Survive* in the moment

2. *Adapt* over time as their bodies and circumstances change

3. *Live a good life*

HELP exists and is valued because human beings are a social species who can't survive without it.

We did not evolve to be capable of taking care of all their concerns, situations, capabilities and strategies without help from others.

All OPNS, and goods and services, HELP people fulfill their intentions, or people decline to buy them.

Human life at home and at work is organized around the production and acceptance of HELP.

The more HELP people are able to afford to take care of their concerns, situations, capabilities and strategies,

... the higher their standard of living.

*****

Reality's Operations

Cause and Effect.

That's it. Nothing else is real.

Aji's Hierarchy of Reality's Operations

3 Fundamental Distinctions of Interpretations

… to observe and interpret reality's operations:

Principles

Laws

Mechanisms

Reality's Operations

Cause and Effect.

That's it. Nothing else is real.

Reality's operations are all there is. They are indifferent to human existence. There is no magic. There are only causes and their effects. How people feel about reality alters nothing.

This is true about making money, careers and businesses.

There are physics: electromagnetism, gravity, strong nuclear forces and weak nuclear forces.

That's all.

And none of them are obvious, objective, permanent or perceivable to our senses or commonsensical.

We have to go to school to learn them.

The universe doesn't care about people, what they know about practical reality or what they feel strongly is fair and equitable.

Human beings are simply a part of the universe that is aware of itself.

Reality's operations don't care:

What businesspeople think, feel, believe, want, wish or hope for.

If businesspeople and their families are rich or poor, healthy or sick, hungry or well-fed, living a good life or suffering.

What businesspeople think is right or what they are entitled to.

If businesspeople are innocent, naïve, wonderful, well intentioned, and righteous.

If they work hard, are determined to get the job done, rely on their common sense and make incremental improvements.

The universe doesn't care about people's opinions, even when they feel very strongly that it ought to.

The indifference of the universe includes the array of vendors who sell what economists call non-discretionary goods and services, i.e., food, housing, medical care and transportation.

This includes grocery stores, utility companies, banks, hospitals, pharmacies, doctors, gas stations and service centers.

Each one is indifferent to the consequences that are triggered when they decline to give people what they need to survive and adapt because they don't have enough money to pay for it.

They don't care, for instance, if you and your spouse are old, tired, sick, in pain, suffering and was a highly valued customer for 30 years. *If you can't pay, they won't help you.*

When businesspeople accept the indifference of the universe and their complete lack of importance to it with humility, grace and dignity,

> … they are more likely to understand why they need to work to earn and save "enough money" to avoid running out of it with their spouse before they die.

The universe, business and the marketplace are rational, not psychological or magical.

> There are only causes and their effects.

* * * * *

Aji's Hierarchy of Reality's Operations

Aji is a business philosophy. It is organized around how reality's operations nest inside one another:

1. ***Physics***   Cause and effect, gravity, electro-magnetism, the strong and weak nuclear forces

2. ***Biology***   We are a social and linguistic species who need help from one another to survive.

                            Our biological structures such as our nervous system determines behavior, and *not* how we think.

3. ***Languaging***   How human beings interpret reality and design new thoughts and actions to survive, adapt and bring the world in which they live into existence for themselves and society

*4. **Culture/history***	Standard, economic practices societies create in specific locations to take care of their most fundamental human concerns
*5. **Social behavior***	Learning, communication, coordination and production to make money, or HELP one another to survive, adapt and live a good life
*6. **Individual behavior***	Interpret life, make commitments and act to survive, adapt over time as our bodies and circumstances change, and live a good life that is deeply meaningful, worthwhile, satisfying and enjoyable

To the extent businesspeople understand reality's operations they are equipped to think and act effectively, strategically and competitively to *double* their productivity, value and incomes.

> In other words, knowing how to think and act coherently with reality's operations to make money when using computers and the internet,

> > *... is a competitive capability used to produce competitive advantages in IR#4.*

To the extent businesspeople believe in magic, are ignorant bullshitters who don't care about what is true or factual, or don't understand that *everything* works consistently with principles, laws and mechanisms we can understand,

> *... they cannot compete successfully against those who do.*

Fortunately, Aji reveals how to think and act rationally in a global marketplace organized around the ubiquitous use of computers and the internet to "make money".

* * * * *

Principles, Laws and Mechanisms

3 Fundamental Distinctions

Used to Observe and Interpret Reality's Operations

Reality's operations -- gravity, electromagnetism and the strong and weak nuclear forces -- or physics, biology, languaging, culture, social behavior and individual behavior -- produce our environment and the different ways it works.

Together, they produce the *threats* we need to avoid, the *obligations* we need to fulfill and the *opportunities* we have to exploit to produce outcomes, fulfill our intentions, survive, adapt and live good lives.

IR#4 businesspeople learn reality's operations when they use Aji so they can exploit the new tactical, strategic and competitive capabilities computers and the internet make possible and necessary to earn a Normal IR#4 Income, or to double productivity, value and incomes.

When businesspeople use Aji, they use three fundamental distinctions to observe and interpret reality's operations.

Principles   Explanations of how complex systems work, such as the economy, politics, demographics, traffic flows, how crowds react when panicked, and how causes and effects cascade in sequences of effects

It's very important to mention that principles such as explanations based on a bell curve often *include exceptions* to general rules. The exceptions are part of the rule and don't invalidate it. They are part of the proof that the principle exists.

The array of responses that are triggered when people are offered HELP they need that is scarce, for instance, *includes* a small percentage of outliers who do not respond to them.

Laws

Explanations about reality's operations, their causes and effects, and the threats, obligations and opportunities they produce, in terms of:

What will happen

What will not happen

What may happen

Or, what is *required, forbidden* and *allowed* to produce an outcome,

> ... that include many outcomes about how causes and effects cascade in sequences of effects

> ... such as how and why water boils

> ... or how and why people always respond to scarcity and marginal utilities

Mechanisms   Simple, digital (or binary) explanations of causes
and their direct effects

> … such as closing an electrical circuit to turn
> on lights

*****

Power

Competitive Capabilities and Advantages

What Is Power?

Sources

Forms

Categories

Operations

Methods of Accumulating

Sources of Power (list)

Locations from which capabilities can be acquired

Power

Business is a game of power.

Whoever has the most power to produce superior outcomes for Buyers -- customers, employers, employees, colleagues and vendors -- or superior offers, practices, narratives and strategies (OPNS), wins.

There's nothing else.

It doesn't matter what people want, wish, believe, desire, prefer or think about it.

It doesn't matter how much businesspeople, politicians, entertainers and reporters complain about it, disagree, argue or think it's bad and wrong.

It doesn't matter how many movies and television programs show how wonderful it would be if self-righteous imbeciles got rich, instead of businesspeople who accumulate power.

The raw truth is that either businesspeople accumulate power throughout their career and produce "good aji", or they get run over by those who do.

   * See **What Does Aji Mean?** at the start of this volume for a description of "good aji".

Those with the most power to produce OPNS others value win the opportunities they seek to fulfill their financial, career and business intentions.

Those who lack the competitive capabilities needed to produce the competitive advantages needed to win transactions and make money in the marketplace, lose and so does their family.

Power is not magic. It is rational. It is the knowledge needed to use causes and their effects to produce OPNS with superior value, or importance, utility and worth, from a Buyer's point of view.

People increase their power, or capability to produce outcomes and make money, by using different "Sources of Power".

Sources of Power are locations people use to increase their capabilities to produce outcomes that fulfill their intentions,

... such as knowledge, money, tools, identities, roles, accomplishments and networks.

There's a list of Sources of Power later in this section.

Computers and the internet are *new* Sources of Power, which is why they require new knowledge to exploit.

They make Sources of Power available to businesspeople and businesses that have never before existed.

They are the best moneymaking tools ever invented, by far.

Their operations in the marketplace -- their capabilities to help businesspeople learn, communicate, coordinate thought and action, and produce fresh, new OPNS -- *can't* be understood with common sense.

* * * * *

Competitive Capabilities and Advantages

Aji is a ***new Source of Power*** and a ***new dominant strategy*** in the marketplace at the same time.

It shows businesspeople the new knowledge they need to accumulate the power they need to earn a living in IR#4's competitive situations.

Since computers and the internet are new Sources of Power to make money that can be used to exploit many more Sources of Power to make even more money,

... it is essential for IR#4 businesspeople to have a working knowledge of power,

... what it is, how it is acquired, and how it is used strategically and competitively to make money.

What Is Power?

Power in *non-competitive situations* is simply the knowledge or capability to produce an outcome, such as knowing how to drive a car safely or turn on a computer.

Power in *competitive situations* is the capability to produce an outcome that is superior to one's competitors, in the view of one's Buyers, i.e., customers, employers, employees, colleagues and vendors, such as designing and executing a *superior* tactic, strategy, offer, practice or narrative.

Power requires knowledge about *reality's operations.*

> *Knowledge*, remember, is the capability to produce an intended outcome in a given set of circumstances.

To compete successfully in IR#4 to *double* productivity, value and incomes, businesspeople need to learn how to use completely new:

1. *Sources of Power*

2. *Forms of Power*

3. *Categories of Power*

4. *Operations of Power*

5. *Methods of Accumulating Power*

Sources of Power

Locations from which *superior* capacities to think and act effectively originate

IR#4 businesspeople use them *strategically* in *fundamental* and *specific* strategies

> … to produce competitive advantages, *superior* value and top 1% annual incomes.

Sources of Power include knowledge or discourse, tools, humility, money, ethics of power, offers, practices, narratives, networks, autonomies, accomplishments, identities of trust and value, leadership roles, business organizations, etc.

Sources of weakness include ignorance, common offers, practices, narratives and strategies (OPNS), task orientation, reliance on common sense, aimless drift, indifference, apathy, pride, ordinary skills, typical language, cliches, ignorance and illiteracy.

Forms of Power   *Practices or skills* people and
                             businesses use to:

                             Take care of *concerns*

                             Produce intended and satisfactory
                             situations

                             Acquire *new capabilities* to think
                             and act effectively

                                   ... such as selling, designing
                                   new OPNS, or using a
                                   fundamental, competitive
                                   strategy

                             Execute *new strategies*, to get
                             things done

Categories of Power   *Groupings of capacities,* such as
                             finance, marketing, engineering,
                             accounting, leading, manufacturing,
                             etc.,

                                   ... in which IR#4 businesspeople
                                   and businesses think and act

                                   ... and transact for help with their
                                   networks when necessary

| **Operations of Power** | *Philosophies, principles, laws* and *mechanisms* that explain the descriptions, meanings, relevance, value and purposes of different forms of power |
| | |

... IR#4 businesspeople use to design, craft, speak and execute offers, practices, narratives and strategies

... to produce competitive advantages, *superior* value and top 1% annual incomes

... such as how marginal utilities and selling actually work

| **Methods of Accumulating Power** | *Practices* IR#4 businesspeople use to accumulate *superior* capacities to think and act with offers, practices, narratives and strategies, |
| | |

... such as learning, communicating, coordinating, building networks, hiring people, selling, designing OPNS, leading, etc.

Sources of Power

Locations from which capabilities can be acquired

Body

Family

Culture

People

Physical Resources

Tools

Discourses -
    Knowledge and skills

Money

Marketplace

Public Identity

Legal Authority

Legal Monopolies

Organization

Force (Military, police)

Marriage

Friends (Sociability)

Obligations - Duty owned

Networks of Capabilities

    Transaction help
    Tactical help
    Professional help
    Collegial help

Practices and Skills

Energy

Natural Laws/Reality's
Operations

Monopolies and Auctions

Declarations - Skill

Narratives

Moods

*****

20 Aji Tactical, Strategic and

Competitive Distinctions

To Double Productivity, Value and Income

The Fundamental Flow of Aji Action Distinctions:

Notice, Observe, Assess, Design, Prepare to Act and Act

The 20 Aji Distinctions

1. *Top 1% Explanations: DMRVP*

2. *Prerequisites of the Self*

3. *Quit thought and action guaranteed to produce bottom 99% outcomes immediately!*

4. *Hold all your purposes, or intentions to produce outcomes, simultaneously, at all times and under all circumstances*

5. *Fundamental Strategy: The Aji Source Fundamental Strategy*

6. *Coherence with Reality's Operations*

7. *Use Aji as your IR#4 dominant strategy, every day*

8. *Practice competitive learning, every day*

9. *Accumulate power, every day*

10. *Organization, Structure and State*

11. *Cope, produce or deal with competitive situations tactically, strategically and competitively*

12. *Produce tactical, strategic and competitive commitments*

13. *Use CDVF for every thought and action*

14. *Produce superior identities (TVAL&D)*

15. *Design steady streams of new offers, practices, narratives and strategies (OPNS), every day*

16. *12 economic principles*

17. *Investing in three acts*

18. *The Spine of Business Concerns*

19. *Produce competitive marginal utilities, every day*

20. *Produce monopolies and auctions to achieve the highest prices and profit margins by (1) being first to market, (2) having the best design, and (3) being the most complex and powerful*

Aji's Tactical, Strategic and Competitive Distinctions

To Double Productivity, Value and Incomes

I came upon this group of important, or consequential, Aji distinctions in my notes and thought it might be useful to revisit them in this format from time to time.

Some of the distinctions, skills and practices are also included elsewhere in the four volumes of these notes.

Use them to develop your *Aji Action Package*:

Ambitions, Moods and Explanations

Distinctions, Interpretations and Intentions

Commitments, Business Practices and Outcomes

Use these Aji strategic distinctions to develop your abilities to notice, observe, assess, design action, prepare to act and act with your offers practices, narratives and strategies (OPNS) in IR#4's rapidly changing and intensely competitive marketplace,

... to fulfill your financial, career and business intentions,

... or to *double* your productivity, value and income.

* * * * *

The Fundamental Flow of Aji Action Distinctions:

Notice, Observe, Assess, Design, Prepare to Act and Act

Here is the fundamental flow of Aji action distinctions to use every day, all day, *in sequence*, when working with the 20 strategic distinctions that follow:

Notice

Bring *intentions, concerns, situations, capabilities* and *strategies* into your awareness by talking to yourself, writing about them, or speaking them into existence with your networks using DMRVP, or their descriptions, meanings, relevance, value and purposes.

Observe

Make interpretations about what you **notice** to determine the real properties of what you notice,

... or how what you are observing affects your (1) *intentions*, (2) *concerns*, (3) *situations*, (4) *capabilities* and (5) *strategies* to fulfill your intentions.

Assess   Make well-grounded interpretations and judgments about what you *observe* in terms of their *threats, obligations* and *opportunities* to help or enable you to fulfill your financial, career and business intentions.

Design   Use the **assessments** you make to formulate new tactical, strategic and competitive *intentions to produce outcomes*

        ... based upon what you have noticed, observed and assess,

        ... and your capabilities to design new OPNS that are fresh, new, highly valued and scarce relative to demand.

Prepare to act   Then, use the commitments, practices and outcomes you ***design*** to prepare to act by:

1. *Learning* how to design and fulfill them as you intend

2. *Communicating* with networks of employees, employers, customers, colleagues and vendors

3. *Coordinating* thought and action

4. *Producing* steady streams of your own OPNS

Act   Use your ***preparations*** to think and act effectively to fulfill your intentions by executing tactics and strategies competitively to produce outcomes whose marginal utilities are superior to those produced by your competitors.

* * * * *

20 Tactical, Strategic and Competitive Distinctions

To Double Productivity, Value and Incomes

#1 - Top 1% Explanations: DMRVP

Descriptions

Meanings

Relevance

Value

Purposes: Existential, ultimate, strategic and tactical

#2 - Prerequisites of the Self

1. Be an adult who is personally responsible for their life, dignified, and not immature and entitled.

2. Have dignity, not pride or entitlement, and financial, moral and family integrity (including saving enough for old age in IR#4).

3. Fulfill your marriage vows and parenting commitments.

4. Move with ambition, not aimless drift.

5. Be physically and psychologically strong.

6. Don't allow yourself to be addicted to denial to avoid responsibility and costs.

7. Be personally honest, not a bullshitter.

8. Practice humility, which is having a modest assessment about your competitive capabilities, rather than arrogance, pride or conceit.

9. Be a market for power, *and pay for it*, not indifferent or blind to it.

10. Allow people to earn your respect, gratitude, loyalty and willingness to honor them.

#3 - *Quit thought and action guaranteed to produce bottom 99% outcomes immediately!*

Working alone

Trying to figure out strategic knowledge by yourself (it's not possible)

Relying on your common sense, or *common* business knowledge, to understand how to compete in IR#4 using computers and the internet

Working with networks and organizations that rely on common sense, or IR#3's *common, obvious* and *mediocre* business knowledge

Task orientation, or working hard with determination to get jobs done, without awareness of, or commitment to, larger strategic, ultimate and existential purposes such as saving enough money to afford old age with one's spouse

Producing "common" offers, practices, narratives and strategies, which (by definition) lack the marginal utilities required to make them scarce relative to demand

Not having, remembering or acting to fulfill your financial ambitions at all times and under all circumstances so you can survive and adapt with your spouse during 25+ years retirement.

* * * * *

#4 - Hold all your purposes, or intentions to produce outcomes, simultaneously, at all times and under all circumstances

Existential purposes give you:

Meaning, relevance, value and purpose, or make your life deeply meaningful, totally worthwhile, completely satisfying (no regrets) and enjoyable from *your* point of view

A sense of *wonder* about all there is for you to learn to fulfill your intentions

Enthusiasm for the work you need to do to take care of your spouse and children

Passion for the future you are producing for your spouse, children, society and yourself

Ultimate purposes, or final financial purposes, give all earlier strategic and tactical purposes their meaning, relevance and value

Strategic purposes, which are the objectives of strategies, or action plans

Tactical purposes, which are the intended outcomes of practices used to change situations to execute a strategy, or to advance action, by:

1. Avoiding *threats*

2. Fulfilling *obligations* to keep opportunities, produce new opportunities and avoid avoidable risks and costs

3. Exploit *opportunities*

   … to advance action, or make progress, to produce the strategy's objectives

#5 - *Fundamental Strategy: The Aji Source Fundamental Strategy*

Part #1:   Constitute life, financial and business ***ambitions*** *every day*.

Part #2:   Formulate ***Philosophies of Care and Competition*** *every day*.

Part #3:   Learn ***tactical, strategic and competitive knowledge*** *every day* needed to think and act:

> *Tactically*, to produce new OPNS needed to change competitive situations to make progress, or advance action

> *Strategically*, to execute, improve or produce action plans

> *Competitively*, to produce competitive advantages, *superior* value and top 1% annual incomes between $400k and $4m

>> … with offers, practices, narratives and strategies.

Part #4:   Practice ***Ethics of Power*** to increase competitive capabilities and advantages, productivity, value and incomes, *every day.*

Part #5:   Design a ***steady stream of new offers, practices, narratives and strategies*** with marginal utilities that make them scarce relative to demand *every day.*

Part #6:   Build ***IR#4 Networks of Tactical, Strategic and Competitive Capabilities*** *every day* with employers, employees, colleagues, customers and vendors.

   Collegial help

   Tactical help

   Transaction help

   Professional help

Part #7:   Increase ***autonomies***, or freedoms, to think and act effectively, strategically and competitively as you need to, *every day.*

Part #8:   Produce *highly* valued **accomplishments** to prove or ground your *superior* trustworthiness, value, authority, leadership and dignity, *every day.*

Part #9:   Establish **identities** of *superior* trustworthiness, value, authority, leadership and dignity with accomplishments and business narratives to lower costs of transaction and increase prices *every day.*

Part #10:   Hold *highly* compensated **leadership roles** to amplify your strategic knowledge *every day.*

Part #11:   Build powerful **business organizations** to amplify your strategic knowledge, leadership roles and the business' capital structures -- human capital, capital equipment, capital inventories of OPNS, operating capital and financial capital -- *every day.*

Part #12:   **Anticipate and exploit** future threats, obligations and opportunities *every day.*

* * * * *

#6 - Coherence with Reality's Operations

Principles
Laws
Mechanisms
    Physics
    Biology
    Languaging
    Culture
    Social behavior
    Individual behavior

Statistics

Costs: Time, energy, money and lost opportunities

Assessments and Actions to Cope with RISK

    Accept
    Respect
    Anticipate
    Avoid
    Reduce
    Counter
    Deflect
    Overcome
    Fix
    Plan for

#7 - *Use Aji as your IR#4 dominant strategy, every day*

A *"dominant strategy"* is the best course of action to take in a competitive situation, regardless of any other action taken by a competitor.

In IR#4, the dominant strategy to double productivity, value and incomes is two-fold:

> #1 - Always use *a competitive, fundamental strategy,* such as Aji, to design new thought and action,
>
> > ... rather than relying on your common sense, hard work and task orientation.

> #2 - Always use *four fundamental tactics* to execute The Strategy,
>
> > ... i.e., design new offers, practices, narratives and strategies.

Stop using IR#3 dominant strategies, e.g., hard work, reliance on common sense, busyness, getting jobs done.

#8 - *Practice competitive learning, every day*

Recurrence
Reciprocation
Recursion

Reading
Writing
Talking
Acting
Failing

Computers

Competitive learning
Communication
Coordinating action
Production

Spaces of Possibilities

Quit *common* sense, *common* business knowledge and *common* networks.

#9 - Accumulate power, every day

Power is *superior* capabilities to think and act effectively, strategically and competitively

> … to design steady streams of offers, practices, narratives and strategies

> … that are fresh, new, highly valued and scarce relative to demand.

Responsibilities
Constraints
Compromises
Obligations
Relationships

Sources of Power
Forms of Power
Categories of Power
Methods of accumulating Power
Axioms/Operations of Power

#10 - *Organization, Structure and State*

Organize the arrangements of components (structures such as people, money, commitments, actions, tools and identities)

> ... to enable the thoughts, commitments and actions you intend to produce,

> ... or that are needed to enable an organization or artifact to function to produce intended objectives.

Use *structures* such as commitments, actions, tools, money, identities, organizations and roles,

> ... whose real properties to affect people's and businesses' concerns, situations, capabilities and strategies

> ... enable you to fulfill your intentions.

Cope and adjust to changes in *state,* or capabilities, that do not alter the fundamental nature/operations of a structure or organization,

> ... e.g., people get sick and tired, machines need to be repaired, cash flows shrink and grow.

* Read the paper *Organization, Structure and State* on aji.com

#11 - *Cope, produce or deal with competitive situations tactically, strategically and competitively,* instead of using task orientation and your common sense

Situations are unique sets of threats, obligations and opportunities for thought and action.

1. Avoid or cope with *threats*, which are Sources of:

    a. Physical harm

    b. Thwarted intentions

2. Fulfill *obligations* to:

    a. Keep existing opportunities to fulfill your intentions

    b. Produce new opportunities to fulfill your intentions

    c. Avoid avoidable costs, risks and threats to fulfill your intentions

3. Produce new *opportunities* to make money or fulfill financial, career or business intentions,

    … by taking care of concerns, situations, capabilities and strategies.

#12 - *Produce tactical, strategic and competitive commitments, every day*

Constitutive declaration	You are hired.
Assertion	I have 10 customers, not 9.
Assessment	My customers aren't strong enough financially.
Promise	I will deliver the device to your office tomorrow morning at 10 am.
Request	Will you please help me explain our new offer?
Offer	I offer to help you finish that errand if you'll help me finish mine tomorrow.
Practice	The "Toby Method" you invented to increase sales is very effective.

Narrative	In the beginning of a project everyone is lost and overwhelmed. In the middle everyone starts to relax. But, at the end, panic to do a good enough job always reappears!
Strategy	Our objective is to cut our costs by 20%. Our tactic is to continually review our costs and expenses every month until we succeed.
Complaint	I'm dissatisfied with the way you kept your commitment and request you improve the situation by tomorrow. If you accept my complaint, I will continue to promote you. If you do not, I will stop working with you.
Apology	I accept your complaint and I am sorry I did that or produced that outcome. I am responsible and promise not to do it again. I am prepared to compensate you for any damage I have caused. What can I do to make amends?

#13 - Use CDVF for every thought and action

Commitments   To produce superior outcomes, objectives and results

Directions   How to think and act effectively, strategically and competitively to produce outcomes

Velocities   Think and act to produce outcomes at speed and amounts required to meet deadlines or to fulfill tactical, strategic and ultimate outcomes

Focuses   What to notice, observe and assess, or pay attention to, in order to fulfill tactical, strategic and ultimate financial ambitions

* * * * *

#14 - *Produce* superior *identities (TVAL&D)*

Trustworthiness	People's sincerity, expertise and reliability when making, accepting and producing outcomes to fulfill their commitments
Value	People's importance (consequences), utility (practical use) and worth (ROI) when speaking and acting with others
Authority	People who know what is *required, forbidden* and *allowed* to think and act effectively, strategically and competitively to produce an outcome in a given situation
Leadership	People who know how to avoid threats, fulfill obligations and exploit opportunities to fulfill tactical, strategic and ultimate objectives in competitive situations better than their followers

Executives -- CEOs, etc. -- lead by helping people with their constitutions, strategies and capital structures.

Managers -- presidents, vice presidents, managers, supervisors -- lead with their sales, production and profitability.

Dignity   People's moral, financial and family
                     integrity and practical value from society's
                     point of view

                     Do they keep their marriage vows and
                     parenting commitments?

                     Do they manage their money
                     responsibly?

                     Do they keep their commitments in the
                     marketplace?

                     Do they make the world a better place for
                     everyone and their children?

#15 - *Design steady streams of new offers, practices, narratives and strategies, every day*

Design offers, practices, narratives and strategies that are fresh, new, highly valued and scarce relative to demand.

Intended existential, ultimate, strategic and tactical objectives

Conditions of satisfaction

Structures for fulfillment with real properties

Directed
Focused
Restricted
Obligated
Limited
Timed
Shaped

Negative characterizations:

Missing
Incomplete
Task-oriented
Flawed
Weak
Shallow
Bogus

#16 - 12 economic principles

1. People respond to incentives.

2. Change happens at the margin.

3. Resources are finite and scarce.

4. Efficiency and effectiveness trade off.

5. Maximum utility.

6. Power is accumulated at the margin.

7. Firms and households interact financially and predictably.

8. Selfish ambition has altruistic consequences.

9. Taxes distort prices.

10. Property rights and enforceable contracts are essential.

11. Laws are essential.

12. Inflation - increase in money supply, tradeoff with employment.

#17 - Investing in three acts

1. Buy something.

2. Do something to increase its value.

3. Sell it to make a profit.

Action #1 - "Buy low": Expend time, energy, money and lost
                        opportunities,

                … e.g., "buy Aji".

Action #2 - Act to increase its value

                … e.g., learn why and how to use Aji to design
                   steady streams of OPNS that are fresh,
                   new, highly valued and scarce relative
                   to demand.

Action #3 - "Sell it for a higher price"

                … e.g., use Aji to double your productivity,
                   value and income by creating
                   monopolies and auctions to lower the
                   cost of the transaction and increase the
                   purchase price, or your compensation.

#18 - The Spine of the Business Concerns

1. *Constitution* (*no* hot dog stands)

2. *Strategy* (a complex action plan aimed at producing an important strategic objective)

3. *Capital structures* used to "make money"

   Human capital

   Capital inventories (OPNS to sell)

   Capital equipment

   Operating capital

   Financial capital

4. *Sales* (produce transactions)

5. *Production* (produce OPNS and use them tactically, strategically and competitively), design and execution

6. *Profitability* (keep costs lower than revenues)

#19 - *Produce competitive marginal utilities, every day*

Marginal utility is the value or benefits that exist on the edge, or margin, and that make an offer, practice, narrative or strategy *un*common and *superior* to *common* OPNS that, by definition, lack marginal utility.

This forces customers to assess value, rather than "price" OPNS, and increase their willingness to:

1. ***Buy quickly***, which produces the *lowest possible transaction costs*

2. ***Pay a premium,*** which produces the *highest possible purchase price*

#20 - *Produce monopolies and auctions to achieve the highest prices and profit margins*

Monopolies are produced by:

1. *Being first to market*

2. *Being the best design* to help people produce an outcome

3. *Being the most complex and powerful combination of new technologies*

Auction types:

English auction	individuals
Dutch auction	businesses
First sealed bid auction	individuals
Second sealed bid auction	businesses

*****

About the Author

Toby Hecht is founder of The Aji Network, a business education company that, for over 30 years in a complex, rapidly changing and intensely competitive computer-driven global marketplace, championed businesspeople's ability to earn annual incomes between $400k and $4m. He is a businessman, and teacher and student of philosophy, history, linguistics, business, leadership, military strategy and martial arts. He has been a top 1% performer for decades.

Together, he and his wife and business partner, Linda, have founded and operated three successful companies.

Mr. Hecht began writing in his 30s when he set out to read, deconstruct and summarize common knowledge found in more than 60 classic business texts used in courses offered by Stanford University. He used what he learned to write and teach new, "strategic knowledge" needed to perform in the top 1% of a newly evolving, computer-driven, knowledge-based economy.

Mr. Hecht served as "key faculty" at General Electric's Crotonville, the #1 corporate business school at the time, for six years and consistently ranked as the top instructor in his field. He consulted several businesses that subsequently sold, earning the owners $8m to $30m.

In the 39 years of leading The Aji Network, he taught 4,000+ businesspeople how to compete for and earn annual incomes, capital-at-work and enterprise values high enough to enable them to live a good life throughout their career and 25+ years of unemployment in their old age.

He designed and taught The Aji Network's courses, programs, workshops and conferences. He has authored more than 1300 papers, produced more than 400 talks and lead over 350 conferences aimed exclusively at enabling students of The Aji Network to earn annual incomes of $400k to $4m.

Today, Mr. Hecht lives on a ranch in California with his wife and dogs.

Additional Aji Background

Aji, An IR#4 Business Philosophy by Toby Hecht

Aji Notes: Strategic Distinctions and Competitive Business Skills to Double Productivity, Value and Income by Toby Hecht

Volumes 1-4

Tactical, Strategic and Competitive Distinctions and Practices

Orientations, Intentions and Skills for IR#4

Aji IFP Instructions and Reflection Questions (on aji.com)

aji.com   Learn Aji, join an Aji Intention Fulfillment Program (Aji IFP), lead your own Aji IFP

Resources: https://www.aji.com/resources/

IFP Resources: https://www.aji.com/courses/ifp-resources/

Made in United States
Troutdale, OR
01/30/2024

17301155R00197